The Event-Rider's Notebook

The Event-Rider's Notebook

Mary Rose FBHS

Foreword by
Virginia Holgate
1984 Olympic Medallist

HARRAP LONDON

To Beverly

First published in Great Britain 1984
by HARRAP LIMITED
19-23 Ludgate Hill, London EC4M 7PD

© *Mary Rose* 1984

ISBN 0 245-54209-4

Designed by Robert Wheeler

Photographs by
Martha and Iian Shaw of Equestrian Services Thorney

Printed and bound in Great Britain
by Mackays of Chatham Ltd

Contents

Foreword   9
Preface   11
The origin of eventing   13
Selecting a horse   14

PART ONE: Dressage
The challenge of schooling   19
The school figures and how to ride them   22
The rider   47
Sequence of dressage training   54
Correct tack and clothing for competition   63

PART TWO: Conditioning
Good stable-management   69
Getting your horse fit   84
Interval training   99

PART THREE: The speed and endurance test
The cross-country   109

PART FOUR: Show-jumping   147

PART FIVE: Count-down to competition   169

Index   185

Illustrations

Between pp. 64 and 65
I   A good saddle for dressage
II   The correct position of the rider
III   The proper position for the rider's arm
IV   Balance exercises on the lunge
V   Vaulting
VI   The position for the rider when galloping across country
VII   Balance exercises through the jumping grid
VIII   A good position over a small fence
IX   The dressage 'outline'
X   Suppleness
XI   Grooming tools

Between pp. 96 and 97
XII   Bathing the horse
XIII   Taking the pulse and respiration
XIV   A fit horse
XV   The beginning of the cross-country
XVI   A good, confident jump over an upright fence
XVII   Two trakehner fences
XVIII   Two examples of a spread fence

Between pp. 128 and 129
XIX   Jumping into water
XX   The drop fence
XXI   A coffin combination
XXII   A confident show-jumping pair

Line drawings in the text

1	The large arena: 20 m. circles	*page 23*
2	The small arena: 20 m. circles	24
3	Turns up and down and across the centre	26
4	The doubler	28

5	Change of rein across the diagonal	29
6	Counter change of hand	30
7	Change of rein within the circle	31
8A	Large figures of eight	33
8B	Small figures of eight	34
9	Three-loop serpentine	36
10	The half-circle and change of rein	38
11	Ten-metre circles and voltes (six-metre circles)	39
12	Leg-yielding	40
13	Shoulder-in	41
14	Travers (haunches-in)	42
15	Renvers (haunches-out)	43
16	Turn on the haunches	44
17	Half-pass	46
18	'Staircase to success'	56
19	Seven basic obstacles	111
20	Spread fences	121
21	Water obstacles	125
22	Coffin fences	130
23	Distances for combinations for trot and canter gymnastics	158/9
24	Simple jumping courses	161

Foreword

To my mind, three-day eventing is the pinnacle of equestrian achievement. For all that, there have been few books produced that were conceived with the novice at this challenging sport specifically in mind.

That was the case, but now Mary Rose, a leading author in her field, has met this need brilliantly. She has given us a book notable for its clarity and its accuracy, that contrives nevertheless to discuss all the physical and mental requirements of both horse and rider. In its general plan, moreover, it is not to be faulted, for it commences with the selection of a first horse and it closes with the ultimate competition, the three-day event itself.

I recommend this book most highly to any rider, that they may at once enjoy its enthusiasm and profit from its expertise.

Virginia Holgate

Acknowledgments

I would like to thank Myrla Bodarke and Mestre Nuño Oliveira for permission to reproduce Plate XXB and Plate XXC respectively. All the other photographs were taken especially for this book by Martha and Iian Shaw of Equestrian Services Thorney, and I am most grateful to them for their help and expertise. My thanks also go to Victoria Regan for introducing me to the Shaws, and to Victoria and to Paula Matthews for acting as 'models' in a number of the photographs.

Preface

The purpose of this book is to provide detailed information about the sport of eventing. It has been written with the intention of interesting and educating not only those who are already active in the sport and wish to advance, but particularly the great majority of riders who have not yet enjoyed the thrill of riding in their first event.

The book deals with all aspects of eventing, from selecting a suitable horse to actually competing in a three-day event. There is detailed information about the basic dressage movements and an explanation of the sequence of dressage training and riding. There is a section on the rider which is specifically designed to help those readers who must work without the help of an instructor for a large part of the time.

Since I have been living in the United States for sixteen years now, some of the terminology in the book may be more American than English, and wherever possible I have tried to use words understood on both sides of the Atlantic, or to give both English and American expressions. One instance that has been pointed out to me, but which I have not changed, is the use of the word FRAME for what is generally expressed in England as OUTLINE. I have deliberately left FRAME in the text because it is more expressive of the concept I want to convey. It is with the whole FRAME of the horse that we must concern ourselves in the gymnastic training of the event horse, and although changing the outline can only be achieved by changing the whole frame of the horse, I want to remind my readers constantly to think of the horse and rider as a 'whole' rather than in separate parts.

The book also covers stable-management and gives a detailed programme for getting a horse fit, and a section on Interval Training, which can be a very useful aid in getting a horse ready for eventing but which I have found to be much misunderstood, at least amongst the young people I teach in clinics.

The emphasis in eventing is on the speed and endurance test, and this book covers the training of a horse in preparation for every type of fence to be met on cross-country, as well as information on how to walk the course, how to ride the course in competition, how to prepare for and ride the steeplechase phase, and how to ride the roads and tracks. There is a section on training the horse for show-jumping and a section dealing with the actual preparations leading up to competition, first of all in a one-day event and finally in a three-day event.

I have presented the information in a notebook form and these notes have been used in teaching my own students and preparing them for competition at all levels, from the very beginner to the most advanced. The methods used have been evolved from my own experience in competition and in teaching from 1960 to 1984 and are based simply on common sense. I hope that the book will help any rider, no matter what level of experience he or she has at present, to train more effectively and to advance in the great sport of eventing.

Virginia, 1984

The origin of eventing

The origin of three-day eventing — or combined training as a competitive sport — was military. In fact, this competition used to be called 'The Military'. The purpose was to test cavalry officers' charges for fitness and suitability. These horses had to carry their riders long distances at top speeds over difficult terrain and natural obstacles, to deliver despatches.

The three-day event in the modern Olympic Games was first introduced at the Stockholm Games of 1912, and was open only to officers on active duty riding military horses. This competition was very different from the three-day event as we know it today, but it was the start of modern eventing.

The three-day event now consists of three distinct phases:

1. Dressage, which tests the horse's suppleness and obedience on the flat.
2. Speed and endurance, which consists of four separate tests performed in succession, with only one ten-minute compulsory break:
   a) Phase A: roads and tracks. This is a warm-up.
   b) Phase B: steeplechase. This is run at racing speed, against the clock.
   c) Phase C: roads and tracks. This immediately follows phase B, is much longer than phase A, and really tests endurance.
   d) Phase D: the cross-country. At the highest levels this will consist of about five miles and more than thirty large, solid fences on natural terrain, and includes ditches, jumps into and out of water, up and down hills, combination fences, and so on, and is a test of the horse's boldness, jumping ability, speed, stamina and fitness, as well as the rider's skill, training and judgment.
3. Show-jumping, which proves the horse's ability in an arena over coloured fences. It is held the day after the speed and endurance test, and therefore also proves that the horse is still capable of performing an exacting test after the rigors of the previous day. Before taking part in this final phase all horses must pass a veterinary inspection for soundness.

Horse trials, one-day events and combined events are all variations on the theme of three-day eventing. These competitions are enjoying a large and ever-growing popularity today because they test the complete ability of the horse and rider. To succeed, not only must the horse be bold, versatile and fit, but he must be well trained, confident, free-striding and happy, both on the flat and over fences, and his rider must be bold, accomplished, well-trained, fit and, one trusts, able to use brain as well as brawn.

The levels of eventing recognized in Britain by the British Horse Society are:

> Advanced Class — Maximum height 3' 11" (1·20m)
> Intermediate Class — Maximum height 3' 9" (1·15m)
> Novice Class — Maximum height 3' 6" (1·05m)
> Young Rider's Class — Height as for level of competition.

The levels of eventing recognized in the United States by the United States Combined Training Association are:

> Advanced Class — Maximum height 3' 11" (1·20m)
> Intermediate Class — Maximum height 3' 9" (1·15m)
> Preliminary Class — Maximum height 3' 7" (1·10m)
> Training Class — Maximum height 3' 3" (1·00m)
> Novice Class — Maximum height 2' 11" (0·90m)
> Young Riders (16–21 yrs) — Same height as Preliminary.

The biggest difference in both countries between the Novice and Advanced or Preliminary and Advanced levels is the speed at which the endurance phase must be carried out, and, of course, the increased difficulty of the obstacles.

Selecting a horse

General considerations

1. Good event horses come in many different breeds and sizes, especially at the lower levels. Qualities to look for are:
   a) absolute soundness
   b) courage (boldness)
   c) stamina and a certain speed (depending on level of competition)
   d) jumping ability
   e) sensible temperament

2. An ideal size would be 16 hands to 16.3 hands, although there are many smaller and many larger horses which have proved highly successful.
3. Plenty of bone and big strong joints are essential. The horse should have good conformation, and be a straight mover. The hind-quarters are particularly important to provide the drive, and a good shoulder with adequate slope to the pasterns will avoid the concussion-related problems common to many upright horses.
4. Choose a horse with presence, character and intelligence, but preferably one with a calm temperament.
5. For the experienced rider/trainer a horse of five or six years old will probably be the best buy. It is to be hoped that he will have been hunted, and will have learned to look after himself, and that you can test his jumping ability in a way that would be unfair to a three- or four-year-old horse.
6. For the novice rider an older, more experienced horse will be a much better mount.

Testing a horse's jumping ability

Provided the horse has had some jumping experience, test cleverness and jumping ability as follows:

1. Jump a combination of two square oxers with a short distance — 21 ft, or even less.
2. Put the horse through a trotting bounce set at 9 ft.
3. Canter another bounce set at 15 ft.
4. Adjust the fences to about 3 ft 6 in or 3 ft 9 in, and close the distance in the canter bounce up to 12 ft or 13 ft, and jump again. This will tell you right away if the horse is quick off the ground.
5. Watch the horse's ears. He should focus on the fence, no matter what the rider does.

The 'first' horse

1. When you are looking for a horse for someone who has never evented you have two choices, the experienced horse or the 'green' horse. I prefer the experienced horse.
2. The horse need not be in the top class, but he should be one with good basic schooling and, preferably, a fairly successful record at the lower levels.

3. He should move well, be balanced, have run over a number of cross-country courses without being eliminated or having fallen. Horses which start falling at training level have trouble ahead.
4. It is best if he is half to three-quarters Thoroughbred.
5. He must be sound, with four very good legs and feet, no bow, no big knee, etc. He should always be vetted before purchase.
6. Disposition is very important. A horse which must be ridden on a bit is easier for a novice rider than one which must be constantly held back.
7. The horse must be a bold and clever jumper. Watch to see how he handles himself through combinations, with both long and short distances. Let the rider just sit there and see if the horse can take care of himself. A horse with a keen sense of self-preservation, who can get himself out of a tough situation without twisting or hanging a leg, is a good bet.
8. If no such horse with eventing experience can be found, look for one that has hunted. If he has followed hounds boldly, has manners, and is used to galloping over different types of terrain (up and down hills, over uneven ground, through water and mud) he has good potential as an event horse.
9. Only as a last resort should a novice rider be put on a green horse. At least choose a horse with show experience, if nothing else.
10. Age really doesn't matter much. The purpose of the 'first' horse is to bring the novice rider along, and give him experience and confidence in the lower levels. Usually a horse of about 12 years old is best.

The 'second' horse
1. For the rider with a few years' experience at the lower levels, who has the ability to go on, a horse of more quality is needed.
2. The horse should preferably not be too young, and should have good experience at the Novice (in the U.S.A., the Preliminary) and perhaps the Intermediate levels, though he need not necessarily be a winner.
3. A rider at this stage needs to get around many courses, learn, have fun and gain experience and mileage at Preliminary Level horse trials and three-day events.
4. It is important to understand that competition at the Training Level and at Intermediate and Advanced Levels are almost two different sports.

The 'third' horse

1. A serious rider aspiring to the Advanced Level will now need a horse with more scope.
2. Again, an older horse with some high-level experience is preferable. He need not necessarily be a winner.
3. The horse's strong point should be cross-country. Maybe he is not a top horse because his dressage or show-jumping are not good enough, but he may be perfectly capable of giving the rider the necessary Advanced Level experience safely.
4. If such a horse cannot be found there are two alternatives:
    a) to buy a horse with the potential to take the rider to the Advanced Level, or
    b) to buy a horse with the potential to WIN at Advanced Level.

Alternative a)

1. Such a horse will probably be a Thoroughbred or a three-quarter or seven-eighths bred. An Appaloosa, or any of the European Warmbloods, with enough Thoroughbred blood in them, would also be possibilities.
2. Absolute soundness is essential. He must never have had leg problems, even very long ago. If you put out all the time, energy and money (not to mention ground-work!) to prepare for the Advanced Level you cannot afford a soundness problem due to an old injury.
3. Good temperament — a horse with an even disposition, a kind eye and a generous nature is important. A few bucks and snorts on a cold morning do not matter, but the 'crazy' horses just waste your time.
4. A better than average mover (but not necessarily a huge stride or a horse that floats over the ground) is needed.
5. Avoid the type of action that hits the ground really hard — the horse won't stay sound with the necessary mileage. Also avoid a horse who does not move straight, or who moves too close, as he may suffer injury through interfering.
6. The horse ought to have proved his ability to perform a nice steady dressage test at Training Level. Steadiness is an important quality.
7. He should also have had some cross-country experience, and at least handled Training Level easily.
8. He should have speed and stamina, and be a good jumper. He needs to be able to handle a 4ft 6in to 5ft square oxer, and also be

careful and clever enough to get himself out of trouble in a tight spot.

Alternative b) — The 'Olympic' Horse

1. A horse with the potential to WIN at Advanced Level will be a phenomenal horse.
2. He must be an exceptional mover who floats across the ground with huge strides and lots of natural hock action and engagement of the hind-quarters. He must have 'Presence'.
3. He needs a very good temperament — he must accept the noise and crowds, and not be nervous or hot up.
4. He must be an exceptional jumper, very bold and very clever, one who can take off anywhere safely, and who never thinks of stopping under any circumstances.
5. He must have courage, speed and stamina in generous quantities, and he should have a 'desire to win'.
6. If you can find this horse you have found an exceptional animal indeed.

PART ONE
Dressage

The challenge of schooling

Training an event horse is a great challenge, and responsibility. The aim is to produce an 'all-round' horse, schooled in dressage up to medium level, able to perform with presence, in self-carriage, the more advanced dressage movements of counter-canter, half-pass and pirouettes at the walk. The horse must show good basic paces, pure at all times, perfectly straight and with good rhythm. He must be accurate and obedient in his dressage, bold and free across any country, and a supple, attentive and careful show-jumper. Above all, he must show that he is happy, must enjoy his work and co-operate with his rider to the fullest extent, so that horse and rider become a real partnership.

Early training

1. In early training use an arena about 30 metres wide instead of 20 metres. Horses need more space when young, and will have difficulty staying on a 20 metre circle until they attain considerable balance and suppleness.
2. Do not use the sitting trot in early training; rise to the trot. Sitting places too much strain on the horse's back until he has become longitudinally supple, and able to relax and swing his back under you.
3. Keep your dressage training sessions short. Young horses become bored with 'ring work' very quickly, and will develop resistances if worked till their muscles ache. Half an hour at a time is plenty at first for a young horse, or for an unfit horse.

Using the arena correctly

1. Riding correctly round the arena involves paying attention to the positioning of the horse through each corner.
2. It involves maintaining the lateral and longitudinal bend and the rhythm through each corner.
3. Attention must be paid to straightening the horse coming out of the corner, and again maintaining the rhythm.
4. The horse must be kept straight on the long sides.
5. Keep the horse in balance, so that the even footfall and rhythm are maintained exactly throughout the circuit.
6. The ability to do this depends on preparation, positioning and then allowing the horse to perform.
7. Remember the importance of the 'half-halt'. Half-halts, even if only very slight ones, are required before each corner, before and probably after each figure (e.g., circle, half-circle, incline, etc.), before and probably after each transition. In a half-hour of schooling there will be a vast number of half-halts.

Making an arena

1. If you do not have access to a proper arena make yourself one in which to practise.
2. Choose a level piece of ground — if possible in the corner of a field or paddock, so that you have two fences already set. If the ground is not level close to the corner, stay in the same general area but define the corners of your arena where the ground is level. The presence of the fence, even ten or fifteen metres away, will be a help.
3. Use poles supported on cinder blocks or bricks to define the corners.
4. Place two canes in the centre of one short end and one metre either side of the centre point. This marks A, and allows you a good straight entry.
5. Make yourself letters in some way: you can use rose cones and paint on the letters, or employ cinder blocks and paint the letters on them, or use plywood and construct more professional-looking markers.
6. C marks the centre of the other short end, the top.
7. The quarter-markers are placed six metres in from each corner on the long sides of the arena. This is the same whether the arena is 20 m × 40 m (small size) or 20 m × 60 m (full size).

8. The centre of each long side is marked; B on one side, E on the other.
9. The intermediary markers V, S, R, and P (which are only used in the full-size arena) are placed on the long sides, 12 m away from E and B.
10. X is the middle point where the lines A–C and B–E intersect, but does not require a marker.
11. G is on the centre line, six metres from C and the mid-point between H and M.
12. D is on the centre line, six metres from A and the mid-point between F and K. These letters do not require markers; they are indicated by a spot on the ground, if at all.
13. In order to remember where the letters go, teach yourself a little doggerel. I start at A and go clockwise around the small arena, saying: 'All King Edward's Horses Can Make Better Fences', and for the large arena I use: 'All King Victor Emmanuel's Show Horses Can Make Really Beautiful People Fall'.
14. Good footing for your arena is essential — it must not be too hard, or slippery, or muddy.

Preparing a horse for dressage competition

1. Accustom your horse to as many different types of boundary fence around your arena as you can. Place pots of flowers along the sides. Practise with poles marking the sides, white pipe, low trellis, or plastic chain-link. At first he may shy, and be reluctant to stay in the track properly, but with practice he will become accustomed to strange borders close to him.
2. Accustom your horse to following a marked line from A to C well before entering any competition. If your arena is grass you can mark a white line. Also practise with a sawdust line, and with a line raked in sawdust. Many horses seeing a marked line for the first time refuse to go along it.
3. Mark a cross at X and a circle at G. Take plenty of time to get your horse used to all variations of markings and boundary fencing — it is well worth while, to avoid his shying during a competition.
4. With the same end in view, park a trailer or a table and chairs, and/or a small tent or a table with an umbrella five metres behind C. This will help to get your horse used to the presence of the judge at C.

5. Practise sometimes with papers — perhaps anchored by a stone, but sometimes ruffled by the wind — sitting on the table at C. All this should help to prevent shying when you get to your first competition.

The school figures and how to ride them

Circles

There are five accepted 20 metre circles, as shown on diagrams (1) and (2). They are ridden as follows:

1. The circle starting at C. The first tangent point on the track of the arena is at C, the second is on the long side 10 metres from the corner (note that the quarter-marker is 6 metres from the corner), the third tangent is at X in the 20 m × 40 m arena or on the centre line 20 m from C in the 20 m × 60 m arena, and the fourth is on the second long side, 10 m from the bottom corner.

2. The circle centred at X. This circle may start either at E or at B. The first and third tangents are on the long sides at the side centre markers, E and B. The second and fourth tangents are on the centre line A–C at 10 m either side of X.

3. The circle starting at A, which becomes the first tangent. The second is 10 m down the long side from the corner, the third is on the centre line A–C 20 m from A (which in the small arena will be X), and the fourth tangent point will be on the long side, 10 m from the corner.

4. The circle starting at X, where X becomes the first tangent point. The second is 10 m down the long side from the side centre marker E or B, while the third tangent point is on the centre line A–C 20 m from X, towards either A or C, and the fourth on the opposite long side from the second tangent point, 10 m from the side centre marker E or B.

5. The circle starting at X in the other end of the arena to that described in (4) above. In the small arena these circles will have A and C as their third tangent point respectively. (See diagram 2.)

   To ride a circle correctly:

   a) Do not go into corners of arena.

   b) Move away from outside track immediately on starting the circle.

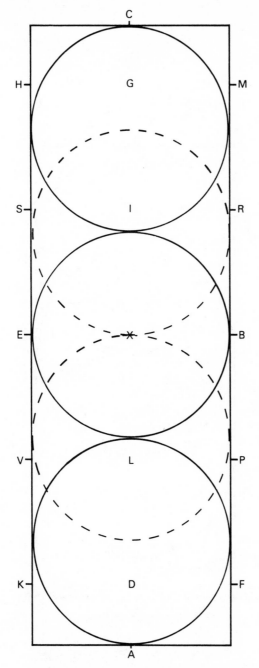

Diagram 1 Large arena – 20 m circles

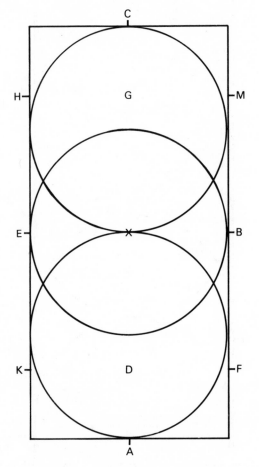

Diagram 2 *Small arena – 20 m circles*

c) Keep the horse continually on the curve.

d) Touch the tangent point for only four steps at trot, three at canter.

e) Look around the track of the circle, and keep your eyes about half a circle ahead of your horse.

f) FEEL the whole of your horse to be on the circle, and that you are riding him with your inside leg into your outside hand.

NOTE: When following the track around the arena each corner should be negotiated as a quarter of a circle. At the lower levels of dressage this circle should be of 10 m diameter; at the upper levels the horse should be supple enough to go deeper into the corners, and the track through the corner should then be a quarter of a 6 m circle.

Turns up and down the centre

1. The horse must travel in an absolutely straight line from A to C. (See diagram 3.)

2. Turn slightly before the A or C marker to merge with the centre line, making the track of the turn follow the arc of a quarter of a 10 m circle at the lower levels. Make the turn tighter at the higher levels — it should follow the arc of a 6 m circle.

3. On the centre line keep an even feel on both seat-bones and in both hands to ensure horse is straight.

4. Do not let horse swing off centre line as he prepares to turn at the far end — again follow the arc of a 10 m circle at the lower levels and a 6 m circle at the higher levels.

Turns across the centre

1. Executed in the same way as turns up and down the centre, but from one long side to the other on the line E to B.

2. The turn should begin just before the E or B marker, and the track followed by the horse should be the arc of a quarter of a circle, so that you merge with the straight line E–B.

3. The horse must travel in an absolutely straight line from E–B.

4. Do not let the horse swing off the straight line before the second turn.

5. As with the turn up and down the centre, the second turn will be in the opposite direction to the first turn, thus changing the rein. (See diagram 3.)

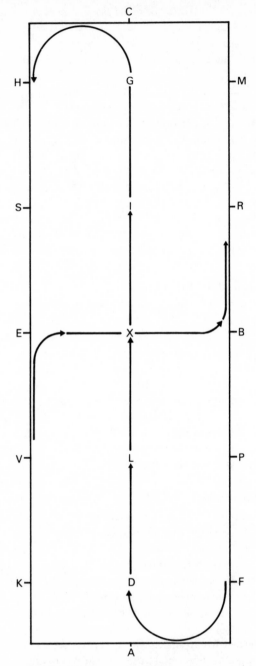

Diagram 3 Turns up and down centre
and turns across centre

Doubler

1. Doubler is another name for a turn up or down the centre line, or across the arena from E to B, as described above, but without a change of direction (See diagram 4.)
2. Doubler and change of rein is another way of describing the turns up and down the centre line or across the centre of the arena, in which the second turn is in the opposite direction to the first turn. (See diagram 3.)
3. These turns are used to show that the horse can bend correctly and execute a perfect turn without allowing the hind-quarter to fall out. In the case of a change of direction the horse must, of course, show a change of bend.

Change of rein across the diagonal (right or left incline)

1. The horse travels round the arena and changes the rein (direction) by following a line from the first quarter-marker on one long side (for example, on the right rein, M) to the second quarter-marker on the opposite long side (in this case K).
2. Line of travel passes over X but will be at a slight angle to the alignment of M and K, since the turn from the track should begin at M, and the turn into the track should be completed at K.
3. Pay strict attention to making good corners, both before and after the change of rein. Keep the horse straight on the diagonal. A distinct change of bend must be shown. (See diagram 5.)

Counter change of hand

1. The horse is ridden from the first quarter-marker on the long side towards X and then back to the second quarter-marker on the same long side. (E.g., M-X-F.)
2. There is no change of direction in this movement.
3. There is a distinct change of bend shown at X.
4. The movement is often performed in half-pass.
5. See diagram 6.

Change of rein within the circle

1. Another method of changing direction.
2. The horse must perform two half-circles, each of half the diameter of the large circle, within the large circle.
3. The horse must show a smooth and distinct change of bend at the centre.
4. The horse must maintain exact rhythm and length of stride.
5. See diagram 7.

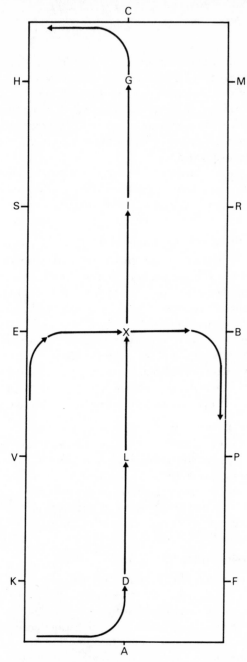

Diagram 4 Doubler

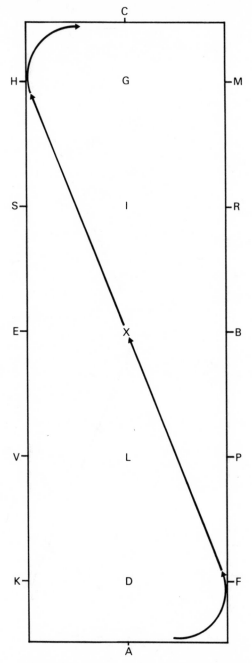

Diagram 5 Change of rein across the diagonal

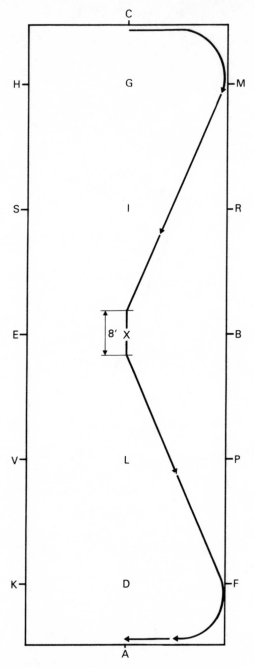

Diagram 6 Counter change of hand

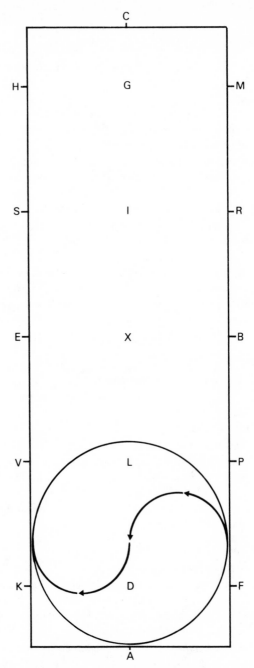

Diagram 7 Change of rein within the circle

Figures of eight

1. Figures of eight are formed by riding two circles adjacent to each other. There is one straight line of one horse's length (i.e., eight feet) where the two circles join.
2. A large figure of eight is performed lengthwise in the arena. The junction of the two circles comes at X, and in the 20 m × 40 m arena the figure fills the entire space.
3. The small figure of eight (or short figure of eight) is performed across the width of the arena, by forming two adjacent 10 m circles.
4. The figure may start at E or B, in which case the centre point will be at X, or it may be performed at either end of the arena.
5. The two circles must be perfectly round and exactly the same size.
6. The horse must show a distinct change of bend in the centre of the figure, and must only straighten for one length (eight feet).
7. A common fault in riding this figure is to show two half-circles connected with a straight diagonal line.
8. See diagrams (8a) and (8b).

The serpentine

1. This is an exercise to demonstrate changes of bend and the horse's ability to perform accurate, even loops, maintaining rhythm and balance.
2. Three loops, taking the width of the arena, is the easiest serpentine for a young horse. (See diagram 9.)
3. The serpentine may have 3, 4 or 6 loops.
4. Loops may extend full width of arena, or a set number of metres on either wide of the centre line.
5. Horse must maintain perfect rhythm, balance and impulsion throughout the movement.

Half-circle and change of rein

1. This is usually a half-circle of 10 m followed by an incline back to the track (at lower levels). In upper levels the half-circle is often followed by a half-pass to the track.
2. The horse must show perfect lateral bend when performing the circle, and become absolutely straight on the incline. If the half-pass is required he must remain bent in the direction of travel. He must show distinct change of bend as he reaches the outside track, and is changing the rein.

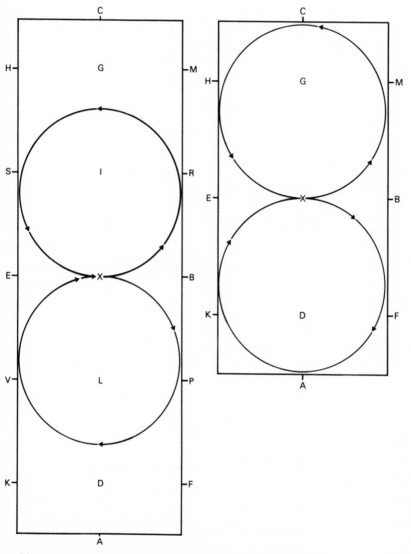

Diagram 8a Figures of eight (20m or large figure of eight)

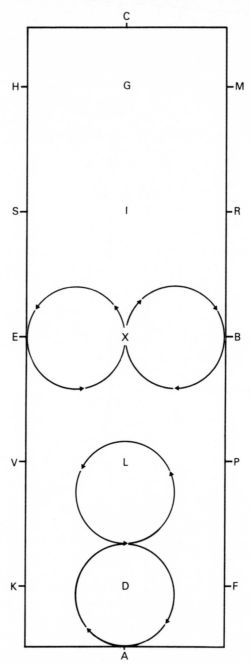

Diagram 8b *Figures of eight*
(10m or small figures of eight)

3. The horse must maintain perfect rhythm and impulsion.
4. When he is more advanced the movement may be performed with a smaller circle — 6 m diameter, which is a half-volte.
5. This is a very useful movement when one is teaching the half-pass as the half-circle prepares the horse for correct bend in the half-pass.
6. See diagram 10.

Ten-metre circles

1. These are executed in corners, or from any straight line.
2. When performed from straight lines, take particular care to leave the outside track immediately on commencing the circle.
3. These are much more demanding than 20 m circles. They require great activity of the inside hind-leg, and therefore increased engagement and impulsion, as well as greater suppleness.
4. See diagram 11 for positioning of circles.

The volte and half-volte

1. Any circle that measures 6 m or less: the most difficult circle.
2. They require impulsion and collection.
3. They are performed in corners of arena, or from any straight line.
4. The half-volte is a useful figure for changing the rein from the corner, or anywhere on the long side. A more difficult variation of the half-circle and change of rein, requiring all the same qualities.

Turn on the forehand

1. Usually performed as a half-turn (180 degrees).
2. Must be preceded by a full, square halt, and followed by an immediate departure at the walk.
3. Horse must walk haunches around the forehand, which remains on one spot, marking time.
4. Horse must maintain exact rhythm of the walk, and on no account step backward, or show the desire to step backward.
5. Horse must be slightly and uniformly bent in the direction he is turning.
6. Rider should use lateral aids — i.e., to turn left on the forehand, use the left rein and left leg, but maintain enough contact on right rein to prevent the horse turning a circle.

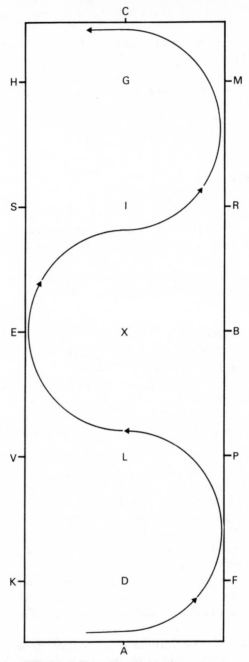

Diagram 9 Three-loop serpentine

Leg-yielding

1. A preliminary exercise for shoulder-in.
2. The horse must move away from rider's leg on a diagonal line, keeping body and head straight.
3. It is often performed from centre line to long side, or along the long side at an angle of 45 degrees to the track with either the head towards the wall or the quarters towards the wall.
4. A useful preliminary exercise for horses at the beginning of lateral work. It is easier than shoulder-in, because it is performed with the horse's body straight — no bend.
5. Once horse can perform shoulder-in, practising leg-yielding has no value. Shoulder-in develops collection, leg-yielding does not.
6. Too much practice can raise difficulties later, when we ask the horse for a half-pass during which he MUST bend in the direction he is going. Beware of over-practising.
7. See diagram 12.

Shoulder-in

1. Performed along the wall at an angle of about 30 degrees (or less, especially in the early stages of training) to the direction in which the horse is moving. May also be performed up the centre line.
2. The horse must be slightly bent round the rider's inside leg.
3. The horse's inside legs pass and cross in front of outside legs.
4. The horse is looking away from the direction in which he is moving.
5. Performed correctly, with the whole horse bent evenly from poll to croup, shoulder-in is a suppling, strengthening and collecting movement. (See diagram 13.)

Travers (haunches-in) and renvers (haunches-out)

1. In travers the horse is slightly and uniformly bent round rider's inside leg. Horse's outside legs pass and cross in front of inside legs. The horse is looking in the direction in which he is moving. (See diagram 14.)
2. Travers is performed along the wall or on the centre line.
3. The angle of the horse from the wall is about 30 degrees.
4. Renvers is the complementary movement to travers, with the tail instead of the head to the wall. All other principles apply. (See diagram 15.)

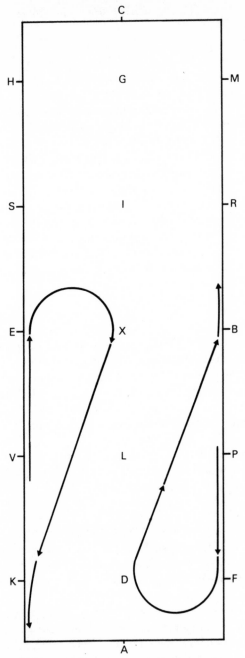

Diagram 10 Half-circle and change of rein

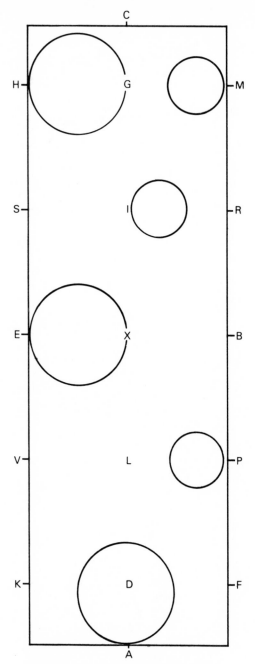

Diagram 11 Ten-metre circles and voltes
(6m circles)

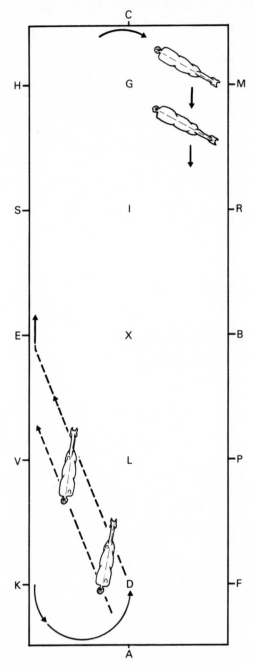

Diagram 12 *Leg-yielding*

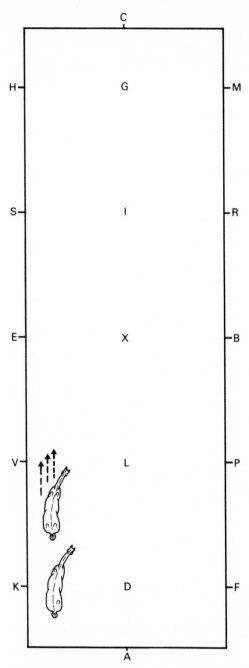

Diagram 13 Shoulder-in

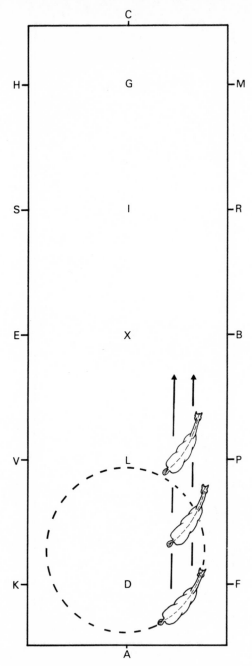

Diagram 14 Travers (haunches-in)

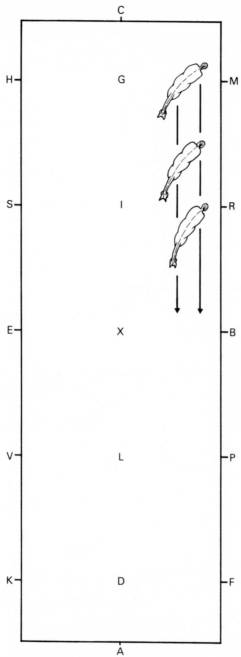

Diagram 15 Renvers (haunches-out)

Turn on the haunches

1. Usually performed as a half-turn (180 degrees) from the walk, in lower levels. The half and full turns at the walk and the canter in the upper levels are termed 'pirouette' (if a turn of a full 360 degrees is performed) or 'half-pirouette' (if the turn is 180 degrees). The difference is that a 'pirouette' must be performed from the collected gait, and a turn on the haunches can be performed from the working-gait.
2. The horse must walk forehand around haunches, while remaining on one spot.
3. Hind-feet should step up and down on the spot, maintaining the exact rhythm of the gait.
4. He should be slightly and uniformly bent in the direction he is turning.
5. Turn may be performed from the walk, without halting first, and this is slightly easier than performing the turn from the halt when the rhythm of the gait is often lost.
6. Prepare the horse by engaging hind-quarters and bringing your weight very slightly back. (See diagram 16.)

Half-pass

1. A variation of travers, executed on the diagonal.
2. The horse must be slightly bent round rider's inside leg, and remain as close as possible parallel to the long sides of the arena. The forehand must be slightly in advance of the quarters.

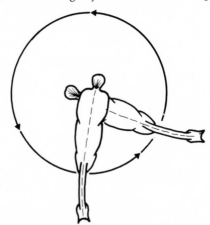

Diagram 16 *Turn on the haunches*

3. The horse must look in the direction of travel.
4. He must maintain the same rhythm and balance throughout.
5. The outside legs pass and cross in front of the inside legs.
6. It is important to keep the horse correctly bent, and also to keep up the impulsion, especially the engagement of the inside hind-leg.
7. See diagram 17.

Counter-canter

1. The horse is required to canter with the outside leg leading.
2. This is a suppling, balancing and engaging exercise.
3. The horse must maintain exactly the same rhythm and length of stride as at the true canter.
4. The rider should avoid pushing the quarters too much to the outside in efforts to retain outside lead.

The halt

1. The horse should stand attentive, motionless and straight.
2. The weight should be evenly distributed over all four legs.
3. The neck should be raised, the poll supple. The horse should maintain very light contact with the rider's hand, and be prepared to move off at the slightest indication of the rider.
4. In the case of a halt in the track at a given marker — for example, at C — the rider's body should be in line with the marker at halt.

The rein-back

1. Performed from an established, square halt.
2. Horse moves backward, moving his legs by diagonal pairs.
3. Feet should be well raised, and not scrape backward.
4. The horse should remain 'on the bit' throughout the movement, and even though he moves backward he should maintain his desire to move forward.
5. He should not anticipate the movement, or hurry in rein-back. He must move straight back, and not swing the quarters right or left or spread or drag his hind-feet.

The transitions

1. Changes of pace or gait should be clearly shown at the prescribed marker.
2. These changes should be made smoothly and not abruptly. The horse should move FORWARD into all transitions (both up and down), and remain light, calm and in a correct position.

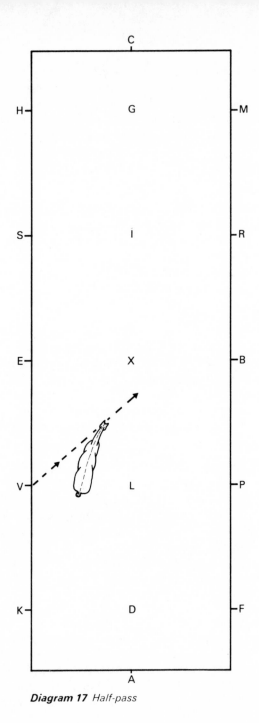

Diagram 17 *Half-pass*

3. The rhythm of a pace should be maintained up to the moment when the pace is changed or the horse halts.
4. Transitions should occur when the rider's body is at the prescribed marker.
5. The above points apply equally to transitions within the gait — i.e., collected trot to medium trot — and to transitions between gaits — i.e. trot to canter.

The gaits

1. There are three recognized gaits: walk, trot and canter.
2. There are four recognized modes of each gait: collected, working, medium and extended.
3. The first requirement in any dressage test is that the horse should perform the GAIT stipulated. If the test calls for 'collected trot — circle 10 m', and the horse performs 'working trot', the mark will be 4 ('insufficient') or less, even if he performs a good 10 m circle, because he was not performing the stipulated gait.
4. Each gait must remain absolutely true — i.e., the walk must show four distinct, even, regular beats; the trot must be a springing gait when the horse steps from one diagonal pair of legs to the other with a moment of suspension between the two; and the canter must show three regular beats followed by a moment of suspension. (It is easy for the canter to deteriorate into a four-beat gait if too much collection is attempted too soon, or if the pace lacks engagement or impulsion.)

General Note

The effectiveness of dressage as a system of training the horse, and the riding of a really good test, depends on:

● Preparation   ● Positioning   ● Performance

The rider

Successful eventing does not depend on the horse alone; it is very much a sport where the horse and rider form a partnership. To train and ride a horse, even in the lower levels of eventing, is a challenging and demanding goal for the amateur rider.

Seat

1. Seat is the basis of all riding. Without a correct position and a good seat there is no possibility of correct application of the aids.
2. A 'good' seat consists of:
   a) Correct position.
   b) Concentration and relaxation.
   c) Balance.
   d) Suppleness.
   e) Co-ordination and confidence.
   f) Correct muscle-development — grip.

Correct position

1. The seat-bones should be placed well forward and down into the centre of the saddle. In a good saddle the centre, or lowest point, will be positioned well forward. (See plate I.)
2. The flat, inner surface of the thigh should rest against the saddle, and so should the inside of the knee-bone. There should be NO tension in the thigh muscles, since this would cause tension in the muscles of the horse's back.
3. The inner aspect of the calf of the leg should 'adhere' softly to the horse's side at all times, keeping just in contact. On no account should the rider 'grip with the calf', neither should the back of the calf come in contact with the horse. Look at your riding boots: there should be no tell-tale grease over the back seam, only on the inner side of the boot.
4. The joints of the hip, knee and ankle should be relaxed and supple.
5. From the hips up, the rider should sit tall and erect, without unnecessary tension.
6. The head should be up, the eyes looking where you are going, the back of the neck against the back of the collar.
7. The shoulders should be relaxed, back and down, the back straight, without undue tension. The muscles of the back must stay relaxed so that the movements of the horse will be absorbed by the lower back and the shoulders will remain undisturbed over the horse's centre of balance.
8. It is easier to keep the legs back and down, with a straight, perpendicular line running from the rider's ear, through the shoulder, the hip and the heel, if you think of your legs as cooked spaghetti noodles (or wet dish-rags), without tension, and yet able to adhere softly to the sides of the horse. (See plate II.)
9. The arms should hang naturally down from shoulder to elbow,

and then naturally forward and down, with supple and relaxed wrists and hands holding the reins softly with the thumb and forefinger closed on the rein, the other fingers curled around the rein, the thumbs uppermost.

10. There should be a straight line through the rider's arm from the elbow, through the wrist and fingers, along the rein, to the bit. (See plate III.)

11. The correct length of stirrup will be determined by the activity the rider will be performing. For dressage the leg should be as long as reasonably possible in order to gain the maximum length against the horse with which to influence the way he uses his body. For jumping, the stirrups should be considerably shorter in order to place more thigh-lever in front of the rider, and to add to his security. For cross-country the stirrups may be perhaps a hole longer than for show-jumping, but still considerably shorter than for dressage. (See plate II.)

Concentration and relaxation

1. Perhaps the most important element of 'seat' is what goes on inside the rider's head.

2. By concentration I mean more than simply thinking about what you are doing. Try to develop the art of 'creative visualization'. In other words, before you do anything think about it, and have a clear picture inside your head of yourself and your horse performing correctly.

3. Once you get on the horse you and he cease to be two separate individuals, and you become one whole. Try to keep this firmly in mind at all times, and it will prevent you from wasting your energy 'fighting' your horse. You do not have to fight your own body; you direct it with your mind, and it obeys you. Use the same technique with your horse.

4. By 'relaxation' I do not mean you to sit sloppily or 'collapsed', but simply to avoid all unnecessary tension. Most riders have no idea that they are tense, stiff and in many cases actually pulling on the horse's mouth. Regular sessions with a good instructor will help you to discover tension in your own position. If regular instruction is impossible, at least take intermittent lessons with a first-class teacher to sort out problems.

Balance

1. Almost all the time the really good rider rides entirely by balance and without any grip at all — even when he is jumping.

2. Developing correct position and good balance should occupy the first several years of your riding life. Depending on the age of the novice riders, and their own natural balance, this development will take greater or less time, but it is an essential step and must not be omitted.

3. Balance is best developed on the lunge, with the help of a very experienced and well-balanced school horse, a first-class dressage saddle, consistent work of at least half an hour every day for at least six months, and the use of balance exercises directed by a competent instructor.

4. Balance exercises are performed first at the halt, then at walk, then at trot, and finally, as confidence grows, at canter.

5. See plate IV for some useful balance exercises.

Suppleness

1. Suppleness is developed along with balance — on the lunge preferably — and by means of systematic exercises.

2. An excellent way to develop both balance and suppleness, and incidentally confidence, is vaulting.

3. Vaulting (gymnastics on horseback) has long been used in Germany for the all-round development of young riders, and is now enjoying tremendous vogue, both in the United States and in England.

4. Vaulting is performed on a pad with a vaulting roller which is fitted with fixed steel hand-holds. As with all riding, it is practised at first with the horse standing still, and later at all three gaits. (See plate V.)

5. Many vaulting clubs make use of a 'vaulting barrel', which is a 50-gallon drum mounted on legs which are welded to it and covered with padding or carpeting. Steel handles are welded to the top of the drum, and much valuable preliminary work can be done even without a horse present.

Co-ordination and confidence

1. Co-ordination of body weight and the movements of legs and hands is essential if the aids are to be given correctly.

2. Co-ordination is also developed by means of the balance exercises on the lunge.

3. Confidence is the result of many hours in the saddle, and is best developed with the help of one or more fairly old, kind, well-trained and responsive mounts.

4. All novice riders should participate to some extent in all the disciplines — i.e., all should have some work on the lunge, some private lessons loose in the arena, some class lessons in the arena, some jumping instruction, some hacking and trail riding, and if possible some exposure to competition by taking part in local horse shows and hunter trials.

5. It is only the experienced rider who should attempt to train a horse. In riding, either the horse must know enough to teach the rider or the rider must know enough to teach the horse: two 'greenies' together usually spells trouble.

Correct muscle-development — grip

1. To ride across country fast and over big, fixed fences demands a fit rider with well-toned muscles. It does not demand great physical strength or strong grip.

2. Grip — that is, the strong closure of the thighs, and/or knees and calves against the horse — is really only necessary in emergencies. Most of the best event riders ride far more by balance than by grip, but all have strong, well-developed leg muscles which enable them to stay in balance with the horse, without hindering him, for long periods of time.

3. In order to develop the leg muscles correctly the rider must spend a certain amount of time working with shortened stirrups in a cross-country or jumping seat.

4. When galloping across country the rider should be up, off the horse's back, and well forward, so that he keeps his point of balance in line with the horse's point of balance.

5. To 'hold' a galloping horse the rider uses the back and the thighs rather than the arms and the hands. (See plate VI.)

Hands

1. Good hands are dependent upon a good seat. Without a firm, independent seat the rider will need his hands to maintain his position on the horse.

2. Once a rider feels confident and secure on the horse's back he can concentrate on developing a soft, continuous contact with his mouth through the reins.

3. Hands transmit the rider's thoughts unerringly to the horse. If he is scared the horse will know it through the feel of his hands on the reins. Equally, the horse will gain encouragement from the

confidence of an experienced rider, which is transmitted through the reins.

4. Good hands give when the horse takes and take when the horse gives, and so the horse goes kindly. But EDUCATED hands do not give when the horse takes; they remain steady, and only give when the horse gives.

5. Wynmalen describes the legitimate function of hands as 'hands may either give, or not give — nothing else'.

6. The hands give the horse light indications of direction and speed, but it is important to remember that they are neither the steering-wheel nor the brake.

Application of the aids

1. Correct application of the aids really depends on the rider having developed a firm, deep, independent seat and educated hands.

2. The key to obtaining the correct response from the horse lies in correct preparation. Take the time to THINK and to prepare — do not suddenly ask your horse to do something.

3. The better the rider, and the more well trained the horse, the less will be the aid required.

4. Always use the lightest possible aid to obtain the desired result.

5. If the lightest aid goes unanswered by the horse, use an immediate tap with the whip to gain his attention, then repeat the lightest possible aid. This nearly always works. Only if the horse is very green, totally unbalanced or very spoilt should you require anything more than the very lightest aids.

6. Never attempt to produce 'performance' without first using 'preparation' and 'positioning'. Create the next movement in the one you are already performing. For example, if you are walking and wish to make a transition into trot, first think about the trot you want. Know exactly what pace and what rhythm the trot will be, know where the horse is going to make the transition, and 'feel' the trot within the walk before giving the aid for the actual transition.

The objectives of training

1. To produce a calm, quiet, yet keen horse who moves freely forward, straight and in good rhythm.

2. To improve suppleness and engagement so that the horse is able to carry the rider with less effort, and perform the requirements of the rider with the slightest possible aids and in the best possible balance.

3. To achieve collection.

The means available to achieve these objectives

1. The circles and circular tracks (i.e., serpentines, figures of eight, half-circles and inclines, etc.).
2. Transitions (both between gaits and within the gaits).
3. The lateral movements.
4. These means are even more effective when combined — e.g., transitions on circles, shoulder-in on the circle, etc.

Jumping

1. There are three stages of jumping from the point of view of the rider.
   a) The first stage of jumping consists in the rider learning to maintain his position and his balance on a jumping horse. The rider should not be given the reins.
   b) In the second stage of jumping the rider should have reins and stirrups and should take *some* responsibility for directing the horse, but should always be mounted on a very experienced jumper, should only jump very low fences, and should always use a neck strap or hold the martingale strap while actually over the fence. This is a bridge to
   c) The third and final stage of jumping, when the rider takes complete responsibility for all the actions of the horse, on the approach, the jump, and after landing. He takes control of pace, impulsion and direction. He should remain softly in contact with the horse's mouth at all times, following through with the hands over the top of the fence. Any errors or mistakes made by the horse at this stage are errors or mistakes of the rider.
2. Riders in the first stage of jumping should always ride kind, experienced, willing jumpers.
3. Being lunged over fences, first without reins and then without reins and stirrups, is an excellent start for riders in stage one. The jump, of course, must be kept very small — nothing over two feet high until the rider is approaching the second stage, when the size of the fences may be increased a little, but not to more than three feet high.
4. Riders in the first stage of jumping may also practise small grids, without reins and later without reins and stirrups. The grid should be in a jumping lane or along one side of the arena, but only suitable, safe, confidence-building horses should be used.
5. It is beneficial for riders at this stage to perform various balance

exercises at the same time as jumping through the grid. This will help them to realize that it is not the rider who jumps the fence, but the horse. The rider must learn to stay in balance with the horse, and not hinder him in any way. (See plate VII.)

6. Riders in the second stage of jumping should be worked through trotting poles, cantering poles (usually cavalletti), small combinations, changes of direction, jumping from trot and canter, gymnastic jumping, and ultimately small courses. (See plate VIII.)

7. Only riders who have reached the third stage of jumping should enter competitions. (There are classes in shows in the USA called 'beginner equitation over fences', and riders in the second stage of jumping could take part in these.)

8. Only riders who have reached the third stage of jumping should attempt to train a green horse to jump.

Sequence of dressage training

General

1. If your horse is to perform correctly in dressage or over fences you must have in your mind a clear picture of yourself and your horse as ONE.

2. Think of the Centaur, a mythical creature which was half-man and half-horse. Become a Centaur.

3. The head and front of a Centaur was human and the hind-quarters were those of a horse, and that is how it should still be. You must be the brains and your horse must be the power, but you must act together as one being.

4. We have three principal means of training the horse: circles and circular tracks, transitions and lateral work. In our capacity as riders and trainers, we should strive to become proficient, and to use all these means to reach our goal.

5. Everything you do with your horse depends for its effectiveness on engagement of the hind-quarters and impulsion.

6. When you ride a dressage test use the judge as your mirror. The comments on your score sheet, along with your marks, should show you where your difficulties lie.

Achieving collection

1. The mysterious 'something' that all dressage riders are striving to achieve is 'collection'.
2. Collection is not an absolute. It is achieved gradually, a little bit at a time.
3. It is possible to be just a little collected, or quite collected or very highly collected. Consider the changing frame of the horse at training or first level, at third level and at Grand Prix. (See plate IX.)
4. Collection SHOULD be achieved by degrees. Do not expect a horse at the lowest levels of eventing to have achieved the same degree of collection as a horse at the advanced level.

Staircase to success

1. Our ultimate goal with every horse we train is to achieve collection in some degree. What exactly constitutes a collected horse?
2. Think of a staircase (see diagram 18). On the bottom step is 'free forward movement, relaxed'.
3. The next step up is 'rhythm', and the next step still is 'Suppleness'.
4. These three steps add up to a 'balanced' horse.
5. The next step up is 'on the bit' or 'on the aids' (which I prefer). All this adds up to a horse who is 'engaged'.
6. Two more steps will lead us to our goal: they are 'straightness' and 'impulsion'.
7. Although the staircase appears to separate these steps, they are of course all interdependent. The separation is only to help in working out a progressive system of training.

Free forward movement, relaxed

1. The horse must move energetically forward from the lightest aid of the rider before anything else can be achieved.
2. Free forward movement is a state of mind in which the horse is listening to the rider and obeying his lightest aid.
3. Surprisingly, a great many people ride their horses all the time, even in competition, in an inattentive state, and without ever really achieving 'free forward movement'.
4. It is easy to check up on this, even on a green or spoiled horse. When you have mounted and gathered up the reins and adjusted the stirrups, and are ready to move off, simply grow tall in the

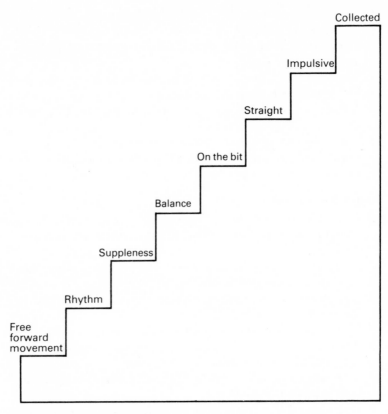

Diagram 18 *Staircase to success*

saddle, concentrate for a moment on what you are about to do, then give a light but distinct aid — just the soft closure of both calves.

5. If your horse is 'forward' he should immediately step forward with an energetic, light and willing attitude. If he does not do so it means that you have failed to 'switch on' to get his attention.

6. The remedy is simple. Apply the aids as described above, but if the horse does not respond follow your gentle calf-squeeze with an immediate tap with your whip. Use the whip behind your leg on either side and hard enough to ensure that you get your horse's attention immediately.

7. Tap the horse only once. He will probably try to jump forward, but you must restrain him. Then repeat your very light squeeze with the calves — being sure to relax and give with your hands. This time he will respond to your lightest aid without hesitation, and you reward him by being ready, and 'going with' him.
8. The state of 'being forward' depends a great deal on concentration, yours and your mount's.
9. You must not forget to be 'relaxed'. The horse too must be 'relaxed', in a state free from the tension of fear or anxiety.
10. A horse who is upset, tense or fearful is incapable of learning anything, and your first job then becomes to gain his confidence.
11. Only when your horse is relaxed and happy with you on his back can you hope to make any progress with his training.

Rhythm

1. As soon as your horse is listening to you and is willing to move freely forward in response to your aids you should become acutely conscious of his rhythm.
2. Most 'green' or 'spoiled' horses will not maintain a steady rhythm, and unfortunately many riders seem unaware of this.
3. Develop in yourself the habit of concentration, so that you are immediately aware of your horse's changes of rhythm.
4. For example, if you are trotting down the long side of the arena, and then as you come to A you circle, you will find that many horses will slow their rhythm slightly on the circle and then speed it up again as you ask them to go large around the arena.
5. If you are aware of this you can use slightly more drive with the inside leg into the outside rein on the circle, and slightly less on the long side.
6. These changes of rhythm become more pronounced the smaller the circle, or the more difficult the exercise — for example, going from a large circle into shoulder-in. However, very slight changes may even occur as you pass through any corner or turn.
7. The rider must monitor every step the horse takes. This does not necessarily mean actively using the aids every stride, but only that the rhythm should be so strongly established and felt by the rider that it becomes an integral part of the horse as well.

Suppleness

1. It is actually impossible to maintain perfect rhythm without the horse being supple. The reason the horse CHANGES rhythm

is simply that he is STIFF.

2. By 'suppleness' we refer to both lateral and longitudinal flexibility of the horse.

3. The horse is a long animal and (at least through his trunk) fairly rigid. However, he does have the capability of looking where he is going, and following curved lines with his spine.

4. The horse is also capable of making smooth, balanced transitions from one gait to another, from any gait to the halt and forward into any gait, and also within the gaits — e.g., shortening and lengthening the stride.

5. This means that the horse CAN BE supple just as a human athlete can be supple, and to achieve 'collection' he MUST BE supple. (See plate X.)

The means of suppling the horse

1. Circles of varying sizes, and all the circular tracks, half-circles, serpentines and changes across the school. Transitions and all lateral movements.

2. The effectiveness of any of the exercises we make our horses practise in the name of advancing their training is determined by how well we ride. It is not possible to apply the aids correctly, or get the correct response from the horse, unless the rider sits correctly and is able to maintain a deep, quiet, firm, relaxed seat under all circumstances.

3. Some particularly useful suppling exercises combine the circular track with lateral movement — e.g., shoulder-in performed on the spiral from a small circle (say six metres), out to a large circle of say twenty metres, and in again. This exercise, performed in walk, can be a great help in teaching a young horse where his feet are, and how to adjust his balance.

4. Shoulder-in performed on the perimeter of a large circle, and interspersed with lengthening of the stride also around the circle (or across the diagonal), is a very useful exercise, especially when it is performed in trot, since it supples both laterally and longitudinally at the same time.

5. The rein-back is a valuable suppling exercise, though it must be sparingly used. If the horse is resistant to it at first, perform shoulder-in, in walk, around the track of a ten-metre circle and then halt the horse for a moment, then rein back. The shoulder-in often breaks down any resistance the horse may be putting up to the rein-back.

6. Transitions, not only between gaits and within the gait but also between the lateral movements — e.g., shoulder-in to haunches-in, to shoulder-in, to half-pass, etc. — are enormously suppling (and incidentally, collecting) exercises.

Balance

1. The next step up our 'stairway to collection' is balance.
2. A horse is said to be balanced when his weight and the weight of his rider is equally distributed over all four legs.
3. Look at a horse grazing in a field, and you will notice that nature has designed him to carry more weight for the most part on his front legs. The front legs are props which conveniently support the horse while he grazes or wanders with long, slow strides and low, swinging head from pasture to pasture.
4. In fact, in these circumstances the front legs carry about 60 per cent of his weight and the hind legs only about 40 per cent.
5. Watch a horse startled by a sudden, unfamiliar sound. He throws his head up, ears pricked towards the sound, hind-legs immediately brought up underneath his body, muscles tensed in readiness for flight. Now he is exhibiting 'natural balance'. His weight is distributed evenly now on all four feet, and he can at any moment wheel around and gallop off, using his powerful hind-quarters to propel himself forward out of danger, at speed.
6. Achieving balance is not quite so simple for the mounted horse. Just bringing the head up will not do it, because now we have the weight of the rider to consider too.
7. The rider adds even more weight to the forehand. The horse has to learn how to balance himself with a rider, and how to distribute this new weight more evenly over his back and take more of it on to his hind-quarters. It becomes essential for him to get his hind-legs more underneath him to help balance the load. This is called 'engaging the hind-quarters'.
8. Exercises which help a horse to engage his hind-quarters are:
   a) Transitions — between gaits, within gaits, and between lateral movements.
   b) The shoulder-in, which helps the horse to step more deeply under himself as he crosses the inside hind-leg well over the outside one, and thereby strengthens and supples the joints and muscles of each hind-leg in turn.
   c) The rein-back.
   d) The turn on the haunches, or half-pirouette.

e) Circles and circular tracks.
f) Cavalletti.
g) Half-halts.
h) Working outside on uneven ground, going up and down hills and maintaining an even rhythm and an even length of stride as he does so.

On the bit

1. If the first four steps have been correctly achieved, step five 'on the bit' or 'on the aids' will be almost a natural consequence.
2. To be 'on the bit' the horse must be able to move freely forward, relaxed and rhythmic. He must be supple, engaged and balanced.
3. To be 'on the bit' the horse must also maintain a light, continuous, steady contact with the rider through the reins. His jaw must be relaxed, as must his poll, and he should hold the bit softly and offer no resistance to the rider's aids. His back should be soft, relaxed and swinging.
4. To be 'on the bit' the horse does not necessarily have to be 'collected'. In fact, he can be 'on the bit' and in a long frame. But to be 'collected' the horse *must* be 'on the bit'.
5. If the horse were 'collected' and yet not 'on the bit' he would be collecting himself against his rider. This is a serious fault, and the result of hurried training or lack of knowledge or ability on the part of the trainer or rider.

The routine of schooling

1. Once a horse has reached this stage of training he will do most of his daily work 'on the bit'.
2. Most horses benefit from a warm-up on a long rein for ten minutes or so, or from being lunged for ten to fifteen minutes after coming out of their stables and before being asked to settle to serious work, but more advanced horses will actually prefer to work in a balanced frame and 'on the bit', since it is easier for them to carry a rider in this way.
3. During your work period each day you will need to allow time for a warm-up and then three or four periods of a few minutes on a long or loose rein interspersed through your hour or so of work. The rest of the time you will expect your horse to remain 'on the bit'.
4. Just as the horse must be completely attentive and obedient to you and concentrating on the job at hand, so you must concentrate completely on what you are doing.

5. Sit correctly, erect yet supple; shoulders, arms and wrists relaxed and fingers lightly in touch with the horse's mouth through the reins. Your legs should be softly close to your horse without ever gripping; your hip, knee and ankle joints relaxed.

6. The horse who is correctly 'on the bit' will have a soft and gently swinging back, the feel of which is quite unmistakable to the rider — even a relatively green rider. Trust the 'eyes of your seat' and allow yourself to become one with your horse.

7. There are no short cuts to 'on the bit'. Some people try to achieve it without realizing the work necessary or following the required progression. The results may fool the inexperienced on occasions, but not for long. Even the tyro will be able to see that the horse who has his head cranked in an apparently correct position, but whose back is stiff and hollow, is not moving freely forward, relaxed, is not consistent in his rhythm, is not supple, and has his hind-quarters trailing uselessly behind him instead of engaged underneath him.

8. The horse brought incorrectly to an improper semblance of 'on the bit' will in fact be using only his legs, without involving any of the rest of his body. This is just as wrong for a horse as for a human athlete.

9. Knowing when to stop and when to go on, when you should ask more and when you should leave that lesson for today, is one of the hardest thing for the trainer to discover. My advice is to err on the side of caution. It may take you longer to reach your goal, but you will not run the risk of hurrying your horse and producing an unhappy, cramped position of his head and neck or an inability in him to engage his hind-quarters and use his back correctly.

10. More advanced schooling should produce a HAPPY horse who is a pleasure to ride.

Straightness

1. Having reached the stage of training where most of your work is performed 'on the bit' you are now ready to advance to the work on the two final steps on the staircase, straightness and impulsion, which together produce 'collection'.

2. Straightness means the ability of the horse to keep his quarters directly behind his head.

3. Difficulties arise because horses are slightly wider through the hind-quarters than through the shoulders, and green riders have

a tendency to line one side of the horse up with the wall and imagine that he is straight.

4. More experienced riders will not fall into that trap. The horse is straight when the hind-quarters are directly behind the head and the rider can feel an even pressure on both seat-bones and an even, soft pressure in both hands.

5. If the horse seems to fall away under one seat-bone, or to hang on one rein, he is not straight.

6. To maintain himself in straightness the horse must have achieved the five previous steps correctly. A lack of straightness usually reflects a lack of suppleness, or a lack or balance, or both.

7. To straighten the horse:
   a) Work to improve the first five steps.
   b) Work away from the walls, using the inside track and the centre part of the arena more and the outside track less.
   c) Use the lateral movements more. Shoulder-in, haunches-in, haunches-out, half-pass, turns on the haunches.
   d) Vary the exercises and combine circles, shoulder-in, and lengthening — e.g., use the shoulder-in followed by a lengthening and shortening of stride, particularly in trot, on the 20 m circle. This gives all the benefits of lateral work, plus transitions, plus circles.

Impulsion

1. Without impulsion, nothing we do with the horse has any value. In the early stages of training we may work without it, but ultimately it is impulsion which gives life to the performance.

2. Impulsion is contained energy, a sense of purpose; it is probably 'impulsion' that we mean when we say 'presence'.

3. The impulsive horse is energetic without being too strong; he is 'in the front of the leg, but contained by the fingers'.

4. The impulsive horse has a soft and swinging back, his hind-quarters are well engaged, he willingly maintains a soft, continuous contact with the rider's hand through the reins.

5. His mouth will be moist, jaw and poll relaxed, eyes and ears attentive, and his movements will be unself-conscious, unrestricted and joyful. It is rare to see a truly impulsive horse, but it is unmistakable, and is well worth working for.

Collection

1. Having achieved all the steps of our staircase correctly, we arrive

at a state of some collection. Now the goal becomes to achieve more collection.
2. The collected horse will be everything described above, and also attentive, keen and pleasant to ride.
3. The frame exhibited by the horse changes as he comes into collection. His hind-quarters will be more engaged, depending on the degree of collection. His top line will appear longer, and his bottom line shorter. His head and neck will be more or less raised from the withers and dropped from the poll.
4. The steps of the collected horse will be energetic, and the energy will be exerted upward rather than forward, so that the strides will be shorter and more elevated than in the working gaits.

Correct tack and clothing for competition

Saddlery for dressage test
1. English saddle (preferably one specially designed for dressage, but any English saddle is allowed).
2. Plain snaffle bridle, jointed or unjointed, made of metal, leather or rubber or of metal covered with leather or rubber, or, when permitted for the test, a simple double bridle with curb chain and optional lip strap.
3. A noseband made entirely of leather. May be a cavesson, a drop noseband, or a flash noseband (a combination of a cavesson and a drop noseband attachment), or a grackle (or cross) noseband. See rule-book.
4. A breast plate may be used.
5. No martingales, side-reins, running reins, or similar gadgets may be used.
6. No boots, bandages or any form of blinkers may be used.
7. A steward must be appointed to check the saddlery of each horse before it enters the arena.
8. At all competitions, saddlery rules apply as soon as the horse arrives on the competition grounds. Horses in the warming-up arenas and other training areas are, however, allowed to wear

boots or bandages, running martingales (and, when they are being lunged or long-reined, side-reins also).

9. Permitted bits are illustrated in the rule-book.

Dress for dressage test

1. Correct dress for the dressage test is military uniform (if applicable) or correct hunting attire. Even at the lower levels the jacket should be black, and so should the top boots, white shirt and stock. Canary waistcoat (vest) and white or canary breeches are necessary.
2. Headgear should also be black, and may be a top hat, hunting cap, or regulation headgear.
3. Normal blunt spurs (no rowels) are compulsory above the Preliminary Level (see rule-book).
4. No whip of any kind may be carried while competing. However, a whip may be used in the exercise and training areas.

General

All tests must be ridden from memory.

Saddlery for the speed and endurance test

1. Saddlery is optional, except that any form of blinkers or hoods is forbidden.
2. A good general-purpose or hunting saddle is usually preferred.
3. A fleece pad or numnah helps to protect the horse's back and to absorb sweat.
4. A leather girth and a surcingle or overgirth is advisable.
5. Only an unrestricted running martingale is allowed. Reins must be attached to the bit or bits or directly to the bridle.
6. Gags and hackamores are allowed.
7. In the interest of safety, stirrup leathers and irons may not be attached to the girth. The foot may not be attached to the stirrup in any way.
8. Boots and bandages are permitted.
9. See your rule-book for more information.

Dress for the speed and endurance test

1. Protective headgear, secured by a permanent or removable safety harness, is obligatory when jumping a fence on the course or in the warm-up area.
2. Breeches and boots, or jodhpurs and jodhpur boots, are required.

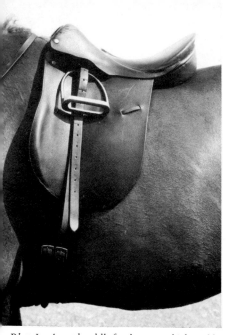

Plate I. *A good saddle for dressage which enables the rider to sit well forward and down into its centre.*

Plate II. *Correct position of the rider – head up, shoulders relaxed, back and down, perpendicular line from rider's ear, through the shoulder, hip and heel.*

Plate III. *There should be a straight line through the rider's arm from the elbow, through the wrist and fingers, along the rein, to the bit.*

A

Plate IV. *Balance exercises on the lunge. A and B. Swinging leg over horse's neck and back. C. Arm-circling. D. Toe-touching. E and F. Trunk-twisting.*

B

Plate V. *Vaulting – gymnastics on horseback.*

Plate VI. *When galloping across country the rider should be up, off the horse's back, and well forward, keeping his/her point of balance over the horse's centre of gravity. This horse's head is a little high, but the rider is in a good position, and is about to check for a fence.*

A

Plate VII. *Balance exercises through the jumping grid.* A. *Arms stretched forward.* B. *Arms to the side. Touching the toes over fences is also beneficial.*

B

Plate VIII.   *A good position over a small fence. The rider's legs have moved back slightly, and there should be a straight line from the bit to the elbow, but she is in good balance and the horse is jumping with confidence and freedom, with no hindrance from the rider's hands or seat.*

Plate IX.   *The dressage 'outline'. A. This horse is showing a good frame, or outline, for the lower levels of dressage. The hind-quarters should be rather more active, taking longer steps under the body, but he is relaxed, forward and round.*

B *This picture of Myrla Bodarke on Brigade shows considerably more collection. The hind-quarters are well engaged and the forehand is lightened and raised. This is the frame of a horse at Olympic levels of eventing or Fourth Level/Medium to Prix St Georges level of dressage.*

C. *This picture of Mestre Nuño Oliveira shows the frame or outline of a horse at Grand Prix. He is performing the Passage. Note the lowered quarters and the consequently raised forehand. The balance and harmony of the highest levels of performance are perfectly illustrated here – note the total concentration and yet lack of tension of both horse and rider.*

Plate X. This horse is showing good lateral and longitudinal suppleness at the lower levels.

Plate XI. Grooming tools set out on a linen Stable Rubber. From top left, metal curry comb, body brush, dandy brush; second row, rubber curry, two sponges, hoof-pick; bottom row, wisp, sweat-scraper, mane comb, tail comb and water brush.

3. Chaps and/or blue jeans are forbidden, under penalty of elimination.
4. Normal blunt spurs may be worn.
5. Depending on the weather, lightweight clothing is appropriate.
6. A long-sleeved shirt or sweater is advisable, as it will protect your arms in wooded areas.
7. A whip not exceeding 30 inches in length may be carried.

Saddlery for the show-jumping test

Saddlery is optional, except that any form of blinkers or hoods is forbidden. All rules apply exactly as for the Speed and Endurance Test.

Dress for the show-jumping test

1. Correct dress for the Jumping Test is military uniform (if applicable) or correct hunting attire.
2. Protective headgear, secured by a permanent or removable safety harness, is obligatory, under penalty of elimination, when jumping a fence on the course or in the collecting ring or warm-up areas.
3. Spurs are optional, but if worn must be normal blunt spurs.
4. A whip, not exceeding 30 inches in length, may be carried during the Show-jumping Test.

Care of saddlery

1. Proper and regular care of your saddlery will not only enhance the appearance presented by both yourself and your horse, but will also add to your safety when eventing.
2. Neglected tack often dries out, becomes brittle and breaks under stress. A broken stirrup-leather or a broken rein could spell disaster for you one day, or at the least cost you a place in the ribbons.
3. Always carefully clean and soap your tack after use. Undo all buckles and stud billets at least once a week, and soap the folded-over parts of the leather at the ends of the reins, cheek-straps etc. with particular care.
4. Pay attention to the stitching on stirrup leathers and reins. When it shows the first sign of wear have the stitching renewed. Regular soaping helps to preserve stitching.
5. If your tack gets thoroughly soaked from riding in the rain, a fall in the water, etc. use something in addition to glycerine saddle

soap on it when you clean it. There are many excellent products on the market to help you put the life back into the abused leather. Ko-Cho-Line is one, and it is a good way to waterproof your tack, and help in its preservation.

6. If you have to put your saddlery away for any length of time clean it thoroughly and then rub a thick coat of Vaseline over it. This also will help to keep it supple and in good shape.

Care of competition riding clothes

1. Riding-clothes are expensive, and it pays to protect them as much as possible.
2. Try wearing blue jeans or bib-overalls over your breeches and boots to keep you clean until just before you enter the arena.
3. Keep your competition jacket in a plastic cover until just before you enter the ring.
4. Brush off mud and sweat-stains promptly after returning home from a competition. Try to avoid excessive dry-cleaning of your jackets, as this takes the life out of them. Much can be done with a good clothes-brush, damp cloth and steam iron.

Execution and judging of dressage tests

1. At the salute riders must take the reins in one hand. A lady rider lets one arm drop loosely along her body and then inclines her head in a slight bow; a gentleman rider removes his hat and lets his arm drop loosely along his body, or may render the salute as does the lady rider. The military salute is only permissible when riding in uniform.
2. The use of the voice in any way, or clicking the tongue once or repeatedly, is a serious fault, involving the deduction of at least two marks for the movement where this occurred.
3. When a competitor makes an 'error of the course' (takes the wrong turn, omits a movement, etc.) the assistant to the President of the Jury warns him (by order of the President) by sounding the bell. The President shows him, if necessary, the point at which he must take up the test again and the next movement to be executed, then leaves him to continue by himself. However, in some cases when, although the competitor makes an 'error of the course', the sounding of the bell would unnecessarily impede the fluency of the performance — e.g., if the competitor makes a transition from medium trot to collected walk at V instead of at K — it is up to the President to decide whether to sound the bell or not.

4. When a competitor makes an 'error of the test' (trots rising instead of sitting, at the salute, does not take the reins in one hand, etc.) he must be penalized as for an 'error of the course'. The same applies for a competitor leaving the arena at the end of his performance in any other way than prescribed in the test.

5. If the Jury has not noted an error the competitor has the benefit of the doubt.

6. In the case of marked lameness, the Judge or President of the Jury informs the competitor that he is eliminated. There is no appeal against his decision.

7. All movements and certain transitions from one to another which have to be marked by the judge are numbered on the latter's sheets. They are marked from 0 to 10, 0 being the lowest mark and 10 the highest. The scale of marks is:

10 Excellent	4 Insufficient
9 Very good	3 Fairly bad
8 Good	2 Bad
7 Fairly good	1 Very Bad
6 Satisfactory	0 Not Executed
5 Sufficient	

8. 'Not executed' means that practically nothing of the required movement has been performed.

9. Collective marks are awarded, after the competitor has finished his performance, for:
   a) Paces
   b) Impulsion
   c) Submission
   d) Rider's position and aids

10. Each collective mark is awarded from 0 to 10.

11. The collective marks, as well as certain difficult and/or infrequently repeated movements, can be given a coefficient, which is fixed by the Dressage Committee of the National Federation or the Bureau of the FEI.

The importance of the rule-book

Whatever competition you are entering, from the very earliest pre-novice test up to international competition, it is vital for you to obtain a copy of the appropriate rule-book. Read the rules through and become familiar with them, and refer to the book often. If you are at a competition and have any doubt about how some aspect of the competition is judged, or what rule applies in any given situation, do not hesitate to seek out the appropriate official and to ask.

PART TWO
Conditioning

Good stable-management

Good stable-management is absolutely essential to the well-being of a competition horse. Without it we risk accident, injury or illness which may put the horse out of commission at a crucial time in his competition career.

Common sense, punctuality, cleanliness, tidiness, hard work and meticulous attention to detail add up to an efficiently run stable and happy, healthy, well-prepared horses. Good stable-management is largely a matter of habit, and once you have acquired the habit your 'yard' will fill you with pride and joy every time you go into it. It doesn't matter how many or how few horses you have; it is very important that the appearance of your stable-yard should be one of neatness and orderliness.

How to reorganize your stable
1. Do away with any junk-heap, or dump.
2. Turn out and discard cupboards, untidy corners, broken brooms, worn-out brushes, frayed halters, old bottles of almost finished oil, medicine, or whatever.
3. Destroy these things; don't remove them to another corner, where your dump will start all over again.
4. From now on, don't hoard useless things.
5. Set out a place for everything. Nails and hooks for forks, brooms, muck-skips, etc. Hang each one in its own place on the wall. You will double its life, and save expense.

6. Always keep wheelbarrows, muck-skips, broom- and fork-handles clean. Wash them regularly. Keep all tools under cover.
7. Remember to hang, and stand, brooms head up, even when setting them aside for a minute or two. Nothing ruins a broom faster than standing it head down.

Stable equipment

Keep head-collars, rugs and blankets, rollers, lead-ropes, water-buckets and feed-tubs spotlessly clean.

1. Wash, soap and polish (you may even use boot-polish) leather head-collars daily. Hang them on polished brass hooks at the door of the loose-box, along with a clean and polished lead-rope.
2. Send winter rugs and blankets to the wash as soon as you change the horses into their summer clothing. Then store them with plenty of moth-balls between newspapers in chests or shelves in the tack-room or store-room ready for next year.
3. Summer sheets made of cotton cost little, keep off flies, let air through and wash well.
4. Horses' coats will never look really glossy if they stand stripped, so whenever possible keep at least a hessian sheet on them.

Stable-construction and fittings

1. Buildings should be constructed of solid, fire-resistant materials, and be well insulated. Brick or concrete block construction is less of a fire risk than are wooden buildings.
2. Roofs should slope not more than 45°, maintain an equable temperature in hot and cold weather, be durable, noiseless and non-inflammable. Corrugated iron, for example, is inexpensive, but unless it is very well insulated it is noisy, cold in winter and hot in summer. If used it should have an inner roofing of wood.
3. Walls should be 12 ft (3·66 m) high and preferably damp-proofed.
4. Floors should be laid on solid foundations, preferably raised above the outside ground level. They should be impervious to moisture, smooth, durable, non-slippery, and should not strike cold to the horse when he lies down. Concrete, if used, must be given a rough facing. 'Dirt' or 'clay' floors are good, but must be relaid each year, as the horse will hollow out the stall centre.
5. The best size for loose-boxes for hunters is 12 ft by 14 ft (3·66 × 4·27 m). For smaller horses, 10 ft by 12 ft (3·04 × 3·66 m) is a

suitable size, and for ponies the size can be reduced further.

6. Standing, or tie, stalls should be 5 ft 6 in (1·67 m) wide and 11 ft (3.35 m) long from wall to heel post.

7. Ventilation is very important. Horses need plenty of fresh air, but no draughts, to stay healthy. Each loose-box or stall should have a window, and the windows should be protected with iron bars on the inside, and should open inward from the top, being hinged in the centre. To avoid having to change stable air too often, thereby causing draughts, allow at least 1,500 to 1,600 cubic ft of space per horse in the building.

8. Doors should be at least 8 ft (2·44 m) high and 4 ft (1·22 m) wide. They should be hinged, opening outward, or hung on rollers. Door latches should be strong, and fit flush to the door. Two latches are necessary on Dutch doors, one at the top and one at the bottom of the lower half of the door, in addition to a bolt on the top half of the door. Kick bolts are often used at the bottom of the lower half of the door.

9. The fewer fittings in a stable the better. Rings, fitted firmly and flush to the wall for the hay-net and the water-bucket, and one at breast height for tying the horse to, are necessary.

10. Mangers should be broad and shallow, with a broad rim so that the horse is not tempted to chew them or to wind suck. They should be fitted about 3 ft 6 in (1·07 m) from the ground, and should have completely smooth surfaces — all corners well rounded.

Stable routine

1. Horses are creatures of habit, and thrive best when kept to a strict routine. Punctuality and regularity are essential, not only in feeding horses but also in exercise, work, grooming and the whole daily routine.

2. Cleanliness is vital. Stalls and loose-boxes should be properly mucked out each morning, droppings should be picked up at regular intervals, and mangers and water-buckets should be scrubbed out daily. NOTE: Always check — look into — the manger before putting in a feed. Some horses deposit droppings in the manger (or water-bucket), and an inattentive groom who dumps feed on top of droppings is not only wasting good food but also depriving the horse of essential nourishment.

3. Passageways and aisles should be swept or raked at least twice daily, and kept clear.

4. The yard should be raked or swept and kept looking neat and tidy at all times. Any grass should be properly trimmed, weeds removed, windows cleaned and cobwebs swept down regularly. Nothing creates slovenliness in the care of animals so quickly as unkempt surroundings.

5. Keep bedding, whether straw, shavings, sawdust, peat or whatever, fresh and neatly stacked, preferably at a little distance from the stable building to avoid fire hazards.

6. Sweep up your hay-loft daily, and do not allow loose hay or dust to accumulate. This is another fire hazard.

7. Keep your muck-heap out of sight, and neatly stacked. Not only is a neatly built muck-heap less of an eyesore, but also the heat generated will kill flies, whereas a spread-out heap will encourage them.

8. Set a daily routine and stick to it. A typical routine might be:

7.0 a.m.	Morning Stables. Look round horse to ensure he has suffered no injury during the night. Check that he has eaten feed and hay and drunk his water. Check for normal amount and consistency of droppings. Feed small quantity of hay and muck out stall. Pick out feet and quarter. Water. Feed first grain-feed.
9.0	Remove droppings. Remove rugs, and saddle up. Exercise. On return remove tack and allow horse time to stale and drink before putting on head-collar and grooming.
11.30	Groom. Put on day rugs. Refill water-bucket. Give full net of hay and second grain-feed.
4.0 p.m.	Remove droppings. Pick out feet. Shake up bedding. Remove day rug, and rug up for night. Fill water-bucket and give third grain-feed.
4.30 p.m.	Clean tack and set fair stable and yard.
7.00 p.m.	Remove droppings, refill water-bucket. Give full net of hay and fourth grain-feed.

9. Routines will vary according to circumstances, but stick to a regular schedule and be punctual. Check your horse as often as possible during the day, but allow him plenty of time for real rest and quiet. Learn to observe him, and always move quietly around him, speaking before entering the box or touching the horse.

Feeding

1. The art of feeding horses depends on a knowledge of the natural history and digestive function of the animal.

2. In the wild, horses are creatures of the plains who are constantly on the move in search of food. So much bulk is required by their systems that most of every 24-hour period is spent grazing.

3. When we compare a horse to a carnivore, or meat-eating animal, the relative capacity of the small intestine is twice as great, and

that of the large intestine four times as great. Even cellulose, the resistant skeleton of plant-life, can be broken down by fermentation and used by the horse.

4. Horses require three main groups of nutriment: protein, carbohydrate, and fat, and also a variety of minerals, vitamins and other essential substances.

5. Proteins are vital for the maintenance and growth of animal tissues.

6. Carbohydrates and fats are energy- and heat-producing substances. They cannot replace proteins, or fulfil their functions.

7. Fibre is a woody substance with little nutritious value. Horses require large quantities of fibre, bulk, in order for the digestive tract to work properly. The capacity of the gut of the average horse is fifty gallons, and good digestion depends on the greater part of this being occupied.

8. Minerals such as salt, lime, magnesium, potash and iron. Horses need these minerals, as well as trace elements of others, and mineral deficiency is liable to affect health adversely. Horses like salt, and rarely get enough. It is good practice to provide lumps of rock salt in all fields, and mineral salt-licks in each loose-box or stall.

9. Vitamins are important factors vital to health, and present in fresh-grown foods — e.g. grasses, fruit, roots, stalks and leaf of maize. Carotene, the matter responsible for colouring these foods and for the blue-green colour of good hay, is convertible into Vitamin A. Carotene is present only in infinitesimal traces, but it is very important. Stabled horses should be fed a top-quality, properly balanced, vitamin supplement (consult your vet).

10. *Rules of good feeding*

   a) Keep mangers scrupulously clean. Allow no traces of the previous feed to remain.

   b) Feed little and often. For his size, the horse has a relatively small stomach, and the natural way for him to live is with his stomach nearly always two-thirds full.

   c) Feed plenty of bulk. Horses have a very large-capacity intestine, and successful digestion depends on adequate bulk. Hay and grass are the main bulk feeds.

   d) Feed according to age, size, temperament and work being done.

 e) Make no sudden changes in type of food or routine of feeding. All changes in diet must be gradual, spread over several days.

 f) Feed at the same hours each day.

 g) Feed only clean, good-quality forage. Horses are fastidious feeders. Musty or dusty fodder can prove actually harmful.

 h) Feed something succulent each day. Grass, sliced carrots, apples, etc.

 i) When work starts digestion stops. Blood needed to aid digestion goes instead to the lungs. After a small feed — two to three pounds — horses may do quiet work, but they need complete rest after a larger feed, and should not be worked fast when the stomach is full of grass or hay. The average time food is retained in the stomach is one to one and a half hours.

11. Amounts to feed depend on

 a) If horse is kept stabled or at grass.

 b) Size, age and temperament of horse.

 c) Work being done and degree of fitness.

 d) Whether it is summer or winter.

 e) What items are available.

12. For maintenance and work a horse requires $2\frac{1}{2}$ per cent of its body-weight in food — i.e., 25 lb food for every 1,000 lb of body-weight — in every 24 hours. Horses in hard work and breeding stock will burn up more food, and therefore rations in these cases must be higher. However, horses are great individualists, and must be fed as such.

13. Most rations relate to dry matter: hay (when hay alone is fed take the moisture content into account — $19\frac{1}{2}$ lb hay gives 17 lb dry matter); oats; barley; flaked maize or corn; horse nuts or pellets (note the protein content, which varies in pelleted complete feed — the higher the fibre content, the lower the protein content, as a general rule); bran; high-protein milk pellets; sugar-beet pulp or nuts (both MUST be soaked for 24 hours before being fed); these are all dry matter.

 Grass has a high moisture content, and is only used as a maintenance ration. You cannot get a horse fit on grass.

14. When a horse is unfit, just brought into training, he will require approximately 22 lb hay and 6 lb grain, preferably in three feeds daily. As he becomes fitter, each week, the ration should change by about one pound, giving one pound LESS hay and one pound more concentrate. By week six he will be getting 16 lb hay and 10

lb grain plus 2 lb bran a day, and by week 12 he will get 10 lb hay and 16 lb grain with 2 lb bran.

15. Times to feed will vary from stable to stable according to working conditions. The main rules are: feed little and often; always feed at the same hours each day; feed regularly, as long periods without food are harmful. Sample feeding is: first feed before exercise, a small feed, 7 a.m.; second feed at midday after exercise and grooming, a larger feed; third feed at night, the largest feed.

16. Water is essential. Clean, fresh water must always be available to horses, both in the stable and in the field. Water-buckets need scrubbing out at least once each day and refilling five or six times a day. No horse likes stale water, and without a constant supply of clean, fresh water no horse will do well.

17. Principal feeding-stuffs are:

   a) *Hay.* Timothy hay, which is a hard, 'seed' hay, is usually best for horses. Orchard grass and brome grass are also good hays. Some alfalfa, or lucerne, which is high in protein and lime and very palatable, is a valuable addition, but should be fed in small amounts only (not more than 5 lb per day per horse).

   b) Good hay will smell and taste sweet, have a good colour — be greenish to brownish, never yellow — feel crisp, look bright and clean. It will never be dusty or mouldy. It will contain good grasses, and will have been cut when they are at their best, between the flower stage and the seed. Good hay can only be grown in good soil which has been looked after with care. It must be cut at the right time, and not subjected to rain, or some of the goodness will be leached out.

   c) *Oats* are the finest energizing food for horses and only the best quality should be fed. They may be fed whole or crushed. They may also be fed boiled (soak whole oats overnight, and cook next day) to help put on flesh.

   d) *Barley.* This is used in many parts of the world as part of the grain ration, but it should not be fed whole, as it is a very hard grain. Whole barley may be fed boiled, perhaps with a handful of linseed, and added to the weekly bran mash. It helps to keep horses in good flesh.

   e) *Flaked Maize (or Corn).* Excellent heat- and energy-producer but low in proteins and minerals. Feed small amounts (up to 25 per cent of the grain ration). It may also be fed shelled or on the cob, but since it is a very hard grain, flaked is best.

Remember that nuts or pellets will contain quite a high percentage of corn or maize, so do not overfeed. Some horses cannot tolerate even small quantities, while others can almost live off it.

f) *Linseed* is excellent fattening food. It should be soaked, then brought to the boil, and then simmered. Add it to bran mash once a week. It may be cooked along with whole barley. Feed from ½ to 1 lb per horse per feeding. It is important to boil linseed (which is the seed of the flax plant), since soaking only releases a poison from the seed, a poison which is destroyed by heat.

g) *Bran* is a by-product of the milling of wheat for flour. It encourages mastication, and adds bulk. Its nutritive value depends on the amount of flour it contains; with efficient milling this is low. Good bran is dry, sweet, flaky, free from lumps, and floury. A bad sample of bran is sour and lumpy. Traditionally used for 'bran mash', a mild laxative fed whenever horses are laid up or on the night before the rest day.

h) *To make bran mash.* Scald 2 lb bran in a bucket, using as much boiling water as the bran will absorb. Cover, and allow to cool. Add salt and a handful of oats and stir well before feeding.

i) *Sugar-beet pulp.* This contains little nourishment, being mainly cellulose with a small amount of sugar. It must be thoroughly soaked for at least 12 hours before use. It will absorb four times its weight in water, and if fed dry will cause colic. Soak only amount required for one day at a time. Wash all buckets used for soaking each day, to avoid sour sugar-beet pulp tainting the fresh.

j) *Horse nuts or pellets.* A compound of a variety of ingredients, including oats, barley, maize, bran, etc. May be substituted in part or whole for grain ration. Advantages include ease of transportation, ease of storage, no mixing, ensuring a standardized, blended, balanced diet. Disadvantages include expense and the danger that the low moisture content may lead to choking or colic unless the nuts are soaked.

k) *'Green meat'* is fresh green food, relished by stabled horses. Vetches or alfalfa (lucerne) are commonly grown close to the stable, so that they can be cut in spring and summer and fed green.

l) *Carrots, turnips and mangolds* are useful to supplement dry food. Roots should be sound and free of soil. Feed them whole or slice them lengthwise to avoid the possibility of the horse choking on a chunk too large to swallow, and not adequately chewed. Feed three to four pounds per day.

m) *A balanced grain ration:* two parts oats to one part each bran, barley and maize is well balanced in most essential nutriments. Black treacle or molasses may be added to each feed at the rate of one teaspoonful mixed in warm water to damp feed. Salt is essential to every horse, and may be fed at the rate of 1 oz per day in the feed, or made available by keeping a block of rock salt always available.

n) *Vitamins* are necessary in order that the body may utilize food correctly. For example, a diet may be rich in calcium, but the body cannot utilize it unless Vitamin D is present. Vitamins are present in most fresh foods, but long storage, poor harvesting, fermentation, too much sun etc. will reduce the vitamin value of feed. A top-quality vitamin supplement is a useful addition to the grain ration.

Grooming

A thorough daily grooming (called strapping) is essential to the stabled horse. Grooming helps to build up muscles, which will be soft and flaccid at first when you bring your horse in to get him fit. Once he is fit the muscles of the shoulder, hind-quarters and crest of the neck should be hard. The shoulder muscles are particularly important, since the horse has no collar-bone and relies on muscles to hold the forelegs on to the body.

A horse in poor condition will have no flesh to convert into muscle, and in this case the diet must be adjusted, and extra flesh-producing foods added in order to build up condition.

Quartering

This is done first thing in the morning, before exercise. The object is to make the horse look tidy for morning exercise. This may be carried out without removing rugs in cold weather.

1. Pick out feet.
2. Sponge eyes, nose and dock.
3. Throw back rugs and quickly brush exposed parts of the body. Remove any stains on flanks, by sponging if necessary. Replace rugs.

Strapping

This is done on return from exercise or work, when the skin is warm and the pores open, and dust and scurf rise easily to the surface. Strapping is the thorough grooming of the horse, and will take an experienced groom from thirty to forty-five minutes. A well-groomed horse is not only a pleasing sight but a healthy animal.

1. Tools necessary:
   a) Hoof-pick, for cleaning out feet.
   b) Dandy brush, for removing heavy dirt, caked mud and dust. Use sparingly and gently on Thoroughbreds or horses recently clipped. Do not use on head, mane or tail. Specially good for care of grass-kept horse.
   c) Body brush, for removal of dust, scurf and grease from the coat, mane and tail.
   d) Curry comb, metal or rubber, for cleaning the body brush. Rubber curry may be used on the horse in a circular motion to remove caked mud and dirt and to bring scurf to the surface.
   e) Water brush; use damp on mane, tail and feet.
   f) Sponges, one for cleaning eyes and nose and one for cleaning dock.
   g) Wisp, for promoting circulation and massage.
   h) Mane and tail comb, usually metal, may be used to help comb out tangled manes and tails of grass-kept ponies, but generally used to assist in pulling manes and tails.
   i) Stable rubber, for final polish after grooming.
   j) Sweat-scraper, a long, flexible blade of smooth metal, is used to remove excess sweat or water, after washing horse.
2. How to groom:
   a) Assemble grooming tools, which should be kept together in a grooming box or bucket. A bucket of water will also be required.
   b) Horse should be cool and dry. Tie horse up short, either in box stall or grooming stall or, in summer, outside. Use a secure ring in a wall or tree; do not tie to fence.
   c) Pick out feet with hoof-pick. Work always from heel to toe.
   d) Using dandy brush or rubber curry, remove all caked dirt, sweat-marks, etc. from horse's body. Start at the poll on the near side and work gradually all over the body, paying particular attention to the saddle and girth region, belly, points of hocks, fetlocks and pasterns.

e) The body brush has short, close-set hairs designed to reach right through the coat to the skin beneath. Start in the region of the poll on the near side. Hold the body brush in the left hand and the curry comb in the right. Work with a slightly bent arm and supple wrist, and lean the weight of your body behind the brush. Use the brush in short strokes in the direction of the coat, never to and fro. After every four or five strokes clean the brush by drawing it smartly across the teeth of the curry comb, and tap the dirt from the comb out on the floor.

When the near side is completed go to the off side and change the body brush into your right hand and the curry comb into your left hand. Before grooming the off side, throw the mane across to the near side of the neck and brush the crest thoroughly. After finishing grooming the off side of the horse, groom the mane. Begin at the withers, insert the fingers of the free hand into the mane to separate a few locks of hair, and brush. Work up the neck, dealing with a few locks of hair at a time.

f) Use the body brush to groom the head. Drop the head-collar around the horse's neck, use your free hand to steady his head, and work quietly to avoid injury to the tender parts and bony projections.

g) Finally, groom the tail. Again, deal with a few locks of hair at a time and start at the bottom of the tail and work up towards the roots. Use your fingers to gently remove tangles before brushing, and try to avoid pulling out or breaking hairs. Do not use the dandy brush on the mane or tail, as it removes and breaks the hairs.

h) Damp the wisp slightly and use it vigorously all over the large, flat-muscled areas of the horse's body. Bring the wisp down with a bang in the direction of the lay of the coat. Wisping is a form of massage to develop and harden muscles, to produce a shine on the coat by drawing oil from the glands in the skin, and to stimulate the skin by improving the blood-supply. Pay special attention to the sides of the neck, the shoulders, the hind-quarters and thighs. Avoid wisping all bony prominences and the tender loin region.

i) Wring out the sponge in the bucket of warm water so that it is soft, clean and damp. Sponge the eyes first, work away from the corners and then around the eyelids. Wring out the sponge again and sponge the muzzle region, including the lips and inside and outside of nostrils, in that order. Wring out the second sponge, and sponge the dock region. Lift the tail as high as possible and sponge the whole dock region, including the skin of the under-surface of the tail. Sponging refreshes a stabled horse, and is greatly appreciated.

j) Dip the end hairs of the water brush in the bucket of water and apply flat to the mane, working from the roots downward to 'lay' the mane.

k) Wash the feet, using one end of the water brush. Keep your thumb pressed well into the hollow of the heel to prevent water becoming lodged there. Omit in cold weather.

l) When the hoof is dry, dip a small brush in hoof-oil, and coat the entire hoof with the oil, starting with the sole and frog, including the bulbs of heels and the wall as far up as the coronet. This improves the appearance, and is good for brittle or broken feet.

m) Fold the stable rubber into a flat bundle and damp it slightly. Go over the entire horse, wiping the coat in the direction of the lay of the hair to remove the last traces of dust from the coat.

n) Replace the rugs, if they are being worn, and bandage the tail, if it is pulled.

Bathing the horse

As your training and fitting programme progresses it will be a good idea to bath your horse from time to time. Racehorses are generally washed when they are lathered up after a race, and if the weather is mild washing a sweaty horse before grooming is an excellent plan.

1. Do not wash the horse if he is hot, sweating and blowing. First walk him sufficiently to be cool; if he still sweats, dry him before the bath.

2. Do not attempt to wash a horse unless he can be thoroughly dried, as horses are susceptible to chills.

3. Use warm water and a 'wash mixture' or mild soap.

4. Use plenty of water. Apply soap or shampoo or 'wash' with a large sponge, going all over the horse's body, except for the head.

5. Use clear water only on the head, which should be washed last.

6. Rinse very thoroughly, using plenty of warm water.

7. Remove surplus water with sweat-scraper, but do not use this on the legs below knees or hocks.

8. Sponge up the remaining water with a clean, damp sponge. Use this sponge also on the lower legs and head.
9. Finally, rub the horse as dry as possible with clean towel, paying particular attention to legs and heels.
10. Walk the horse dry in sunshine if possible. If it is breezy or cool, put a sweat-sheet or wool cooler on the horse until he is completely dry.
11. When he is dry, brush him all over with body brush.
12. A bath will clean your horse, but it is not a short cut to good grooming. A daily strapping is essential to promote circulation, develop muscle and maintain condition as well as to improve appearance.

Care of the teeth

The horse has two types of teeth: incisors, or biting teeth, situated at the front of his mouth, and molars, or grinding teeth, situated on either side of his jawbone and sometimes called 'cheek teeth'. He develops two sets of teeth:
● Temporary (also called milk teeth or deciduous teeth)
● Permanent teeth.

Molars

1. There are twelve in each jaw — six each side.
2. In temporary dentition, there are only six — three each side.
3. Molars form the sides of the dental arch — cheek teeth.

Incisors

1. There are six incisors in each jaw.
2. There are also six temporary incisors.
3. The incisor teeth are situated in the front of the mouth.

Temporary teeth

Temporary, or milk, teeth are smaller and whiter than permanent teeth.

Permanent teeth

Permanent teeth are larger than the temporaries, and yellowish in colour.

Tushes or canine teeth

1. The adult male horse has two canine teeth in each jaw; they do not usually occur in the female.

2. Tushes, or canine teeth, are situated in the space between the incisors and the molars.
3. Tushes appear at 3½ to 4 years, and are fully developed at 4½ to 5 years.

Wolf teeth

1. Molar-type teeth which frequently occur in the upper jaw, just in front of the molars.
2. Wolf teeth have little root; they are vestigial first premolars.
3. Wolf teeth may erupt during the first six months, and are often shed at the same time as the milk teeth behind them.
4. If not shed, wolf teeth may remain indefinitely. It is probably best to have them removed by the horse dentist or veterinary surgeon, when floating the teeth (see opposite).

Digestion

Teeth are far more important to the digestive process of the horse than they are to the digestive process of man. Since the horse's stomach is relatively small compared with the size of the animal, the teeth must grind the food down to small particles, which are then mixed with large quantities of saliva rich in enzymes. The digestive process starts in the mouth.

1. The horse brings grass, hay or grain into his mouth — selecting it with his lips and attacking it with his incisors.
2. The grinding molars are then set in motion. Enormously powerful jaw muscles move the lower jaw up and down and from side to side, creating a rotation action.
3. The food, ground and mixed with saliva, makes its way up the eight to ten inch channel to the top of the oesophagus and then down to the stomach.
4. Thanks to the interwoven enamel and dentine, the grinding surfaces of the molars are kept continuously rough.
5. Unfortunately, the upper jaw is wider than the lower one, the molars do not overlap perfectly, and therefore do not wear down absolutely evenly. As the jaw travels from side to side, and the molars grind against each other, the lower ones do not quite reach the outer edge of the upper molars, and conversely the upper molars never reach the inner edge of the lower molars.
6. The rest of the teeth wear down, but the outside edge of the upper arcade and the inside edge of the lower arcade become longer and sharper.

7. This enamel ridge can lacerate the cheeks and tongue, and may in neglected cases cause the horse such pain that he will hardly eat at all. His disposition, and also his digestion, may well be affected.
8. The remedy is simple and relatively painless. With special files and the right technique a vet or an equine dentist can smooth out the sharp ridges and points, levelling them with the rest of the teeth. This is called floating (or rasping), and will probably need to be done once a year.
9. Younger horses (rather than older ones), usually have a greater need of dental care. Milk teeth are soft and wear down quickly, forming sharp ridges quite quickly.
10. To avoid dental problems, have your horse's teeth checked twice a year, and floated as necessary.

Internal parasites
Various internal parasites affect horses:
1. Bots (the larvae of the gadfly, a brownish-yellowish hairy fly about two-thirds of an inch long).
2. Large and small strongyles, also known as Red Worms and Blood Worms.
3. Ascarids, yellowish-white worms, six to twelve inches long and the thickness of a pencil. Mostly present in foals and young horses.

Effective control
1. Keeping pastures clean and mowed, not over-grazing, and resting or rotating grazing land.
2. Treating all horses every six to eight weeks with effective medication, under the guidance of a veterinary surgeon.
3. Providing darkened shelters for horses in pasture during the gadfly (botfly) season.
4. Removing bot eggs from hairs on horses' legs, chest, neck, on a regular basis, at least twice a week.

Administration of worm medication
1. By stomach tube. This must be done by a vet, and although it is very effective it is more costly and sometimes more stressful than other methods. It is advisable to 'tube' once a year, and to use other medications in between.
2. Paste wormer. Many manufacturers prepare and market single-dose syringes which are very easy for the owner to administer.

Effectiveness may be diminished by the dilution of the medication which takes place in the mouth and oesophagus.

3. Liquid wormer, mixed with feed. This is very effective if the horse will eat it; some horses will and some won't. Watch the horse to make sure the medication is actually swallowed.

4. Powders and granules. Again, effective if horse will actually eat them. Useful to alternate with paste wormer.

5. Injectable wormer. There is now a very effective injectable medication which not only kills adult worms but also the migrating larvae inside the horse. This must be administered at present by a vet, but it is less expensive than tube worming, and less traumatic for the horse, as well as being more effective.

Care of the feet and shoeing

If the horse has been turned out for a rest, and is being brought in to begin getting fit for the competition season, he may have been without shoes all round, or with grass tips in front. It is wise to get him shod during the pre-work week.

Watch the horse being shod if possible, and note any tell-tale red patches near the heels, which could mean old bruises, or new ones forming. Corns and bruises cause much lameness, and a horse can bruise a foot at grass as easily as he can when stabled.

The best type of shoe for a horse expected to perform in the disciplines of an event horse is a hunter-type shoe of concave iron (which means the surface next to the foot is wider than the surface touching the ground), with fullering (a groove for the nails) and, if you have to work on paved roads, with non-slip studs.

Nearer to competition time you will need shoes with appropriately drilled stud-holes so that you can screw in the appropriate type of studs for the dressage, the cross-country and the show-jumping phases. Making these threaded stud-holes is expensive, however, so do not have them drilled until you are ready to use the studs.

Getting your horse fit

Bringing a horse back to work after rest depends on many factors. Each horse is an individual and you must learn how to read the signals of your own mount. Consider how long he was out of work, whether he had complete rest, perhaps being turned out on a large acreage for one or two months. It may be that he only had complete rest for a week or two, and after that was returned to some walking exercise daily, along with daily turnout.

Ideally, each horse requires a rest and holiday for part of every year. When this rest occurs depends on the work he does. For example, a hunter will be working during the winter, and will therefore get his rest during the hot summer months. He will probably appreciate being kept indoors during the heat of the day and turned out during the cool nights. At the very least, he will require a run-in shed where he can escape from the flies.

Most event horses will be working in the spring and autumn and will rest either mid-summer or in the winter. If you want to event at the end of April or early in May you need to bring your horse up in January.

First week

1. A horse straight off grass and from a long rest will be absolutely soft.
2. Walking exercise only, for twenty minutes the first day, half an hour the second day.
3. Build up to one hour of steady walking by the end of the first week.
4. Even though the horse may seem keen to go on and to trot, do not allow him out of a walk. He will settle in a day or two.

Necessity for walk

The horse's muscles must adjust themselves to the weight of the rider and a saddle on his back. The centre of balance is altered, and if the horse is allowed to trot or canter the tendons and ligaments may over-stretch and not return to normal. This could result in strained tendons or ligaments.

Necessity for turn-out

The horse should, if at all possible, be turned out each day for two or three hours in addition to the mounted, walking exercise. This allows him to let off steam by cantering and bucking comparatively safely. In winter this may be difficult, but it can usually be done by using a turn-out blanket or New Zealand rug. In summer (horses brought up in June for the autumn events) horses do best if they are turned out during the night and brought in early in the morning and kept in the rest of the day. Horses will walk quietly if they are worked early in the morning when it is cool, and there are not many flies about. They can receive their feeds in the stable during the day.

Second week

1. After one week the horse should have one day off work. During the early weeks this can be a day in the field (if stabled at night). Horses stabled at all times should be hand walked, led out to graze in a halter for at least twenty minutes (not more than forty minutes).
2. Walking exercise continues through the second week. Make the horse walk properly; do not slop along. Stay alert yourself, and keep horse walking up to the bit. Give some periods of loose-rein walk for two or three minutes every fifteen minutes or so.
3. Dragging feet are bad — they get bruised and scraped, and the horse's muscles are not being worked properly. Make the horse march along, picking his feet up and putting them down firmly.
4. Stumbles lead to falls, and strained tendons and ligaments from sudden jarring as a toe catches in the ground.
5. The first day of the second week about 45 to 50 minutes will be sufficient.
6. By mid-week longer rides can start. A full 6 to 8-mile circuit lasting an hour and a quarter up to an hour and a half can be tried.
7. The horse should return to the stable as fresh as he left.
8. By the end of the second week he should have ceased to puff at the walk and be capable of walking out for the whole ride.
9. Use roads with good surfaces and lanes or dirt roads with sound going.
10. If crossing a field enables you to link up a new ride, and the footing is good and the horse willing to walk and stay calm, then use the field, but on no account trot or canter yet.

Third week

With the two vital first weeks of walking behind you, trotting can now be introduced.

1. Start carefully — trotting jars the horse's legs.
2. Trotting should always be done at an even pace with a long stride, which is less jarring to the horse's legs than a short, stabbing one.
3. ALWAYS WALK THE FIRST HALF-MILE. Even when your horse is completely fit he needs to walk at least half a mile, whether hacking or schooling, before starting to trot.

4. After walking at least half a mile, trot a short distance (from one telegraph pole to the next), then walk again.
5. The first day of the third week should include three or four short trots.
6. On the second day the horse can trot slightly longer spells.
7. By the end of the week he should not be feeling tired at the end of the ride, which should last about an hour and a half and include at least four spells of trotting of a minute or two each.
8. Sound grass verges or along the side of a field are good places to trot to reduce jarring, but be careful not to let the horse canter yet.

Lungeing
1. Lungeing normally means trotting, and so cannot be introduced until the third week.
2. Lungeing puts a certain strain on the horse until his muscles have stretched enough to allow him to circle.
3. Walking on the lunge the first day is best, if the horse will do it. If not, keep the lungeing to five minutes each way.
4. As the days progress, increase the time spent lungeing. Never exceed fifteen minutes during the first week of lungeing, and split this into three short periods in each direction ($2\frac{1}{2}$ minutes each), so that you are stretching the muscles of the back evenly.
5. Do not use side reins, chambons, or any other equipment in the early stages, as this puts too much strain on the neck and back muscles.
6. When to lunge is the next point. I recommend lungeing in the afternoon, having exercised and/or schooled in the morning. This splits up the exercise, and does not tire the horse. Lungeing in this way enables the horse to have one and a half hour's exercise in the morning, and then gradually to build up to two hours by adding a half-hour on the lunge in the afternoon.

Schooling
1. Schooling can start in this third week.
2. Start with slow trotting on large circles. Do not use sitting trot until the horse is much harder; always rise.
3. Start with slow, rhythmic trotting — large circles to right and left.
4. Schooling can be done during the morning exercise if a suitable corner of a field can be found that has good footing.

Exercise only one part of the picture

Getting your horse fit depends not only on correct exercise but also on correct diet and good grooming. Good stable-management is essential, including care of horse's feet, teeth and a good working programme. It is recommended that the reader refer in depth to the section on Good Stable-management (pp. 69–84).

Diet

With work comes the need for more food. When the work moves from the LIGHT category into the MEDIUM or HEAVY category the food must be higher in protein.

Light work is one hour per day.
Medium work is one and a half to two hours of not too hard work.
Heavy work is anything over this, or a very vigorous one and a half to two hours.

Thirty to forty minutes of hard schooling is worth two hours of hacking. Consider the TYPE of work you are doing as well as the TIME.

A *small horse* is 15 hands and will require overall less food for the same work.
A *large horse* is 16 hands plus and will require more food for the same work.
A *very large horse* from 17 hands on up will consume even more.
A *big-framed horse* on short legs will require more than a small-framed horse of the same height.

A horse's stomach is small for its size and lies next to the diaphragm — too much bulk in the diet increases pressure on the diaphragm and cuts down the room for lung-expansion. Cut down the power of breathing freely and you impose a strain on the heart, which lies to the left-hand side of the chest cavity, just in front of the girth area. Heart strength lies in muscle power — the heart is a muscle which circulates the blood. Poor muscle, poor heart-function.

To build muscle one requires

1. Adequate protein.
2. Necessary vitamins and minerals
3. Correct amount of sound, sensible exercise.
4. Thorough daily grooming.

Bulk versus 'short' feed

1. The fitter the horse the less bulk food it requires, and the more

'short' feed. 'Short' feed is packed with energy-producing nourishment — oats, high-protein pellets, milk pellets, maize, linseed are all energy-producing foods.
2. Spring grass and hay may be rich in protein, but are bulk foods, and not sufficient to get a horse fit.
3. Grass in winter has no real feeding value.
4. Poor hay has no feeding value.
5. Always feed only the best, and feed little and often rather than one large feed.

Body-weight and daily feed requirements

Feed according to body-weight rather than height. The following chart gives approximate average weights for heights and necessary daily food intake. Remember that height versus weight is not always accurate — a 14-hand show pony will weigh considerably less than a 14-hand Welsh Cob. Use a weight tape or stand your horse on a weighbridge to determine accurate weight.

Body-weight in relation to daily food requirements of ponies and horses

Size (hands high)	Average approximate body-weight (lb)	Daily food intake (lb)
13	500	12
13.2	600	15
14	700	17
14.2	800	20
15	950	23
15	1,100 (Q.H. or Half-bred)	27
15.2	1,000 (T.B.)	25
15.2	1,250 (Hunter)	31
16	1,100 (T.B.)	28
16 and over	1,400 (Hunter)	35

Diet plays a large part in getting any horse fit. To work a horse requires $2\frac{1}{2}$ per cent of his body-weight in food — that is, 25 lb of food for every 1,000 lb of body-weight. Hard work or breeding-stock will require more.

Concentrates are essential for any horse in serious work, but roughage is also essential for digestion. The rule is to decrease bulk (roughage) foods as the concentrates are increased with increased work.

Never take the ratio beyond 40 per cent roughage to 60 per cent concentrate.

Progressive feeding chart for T.B. type horse, 16 h.h. being brought up from rest and getting fit

Week	1	2	3	4	5	6	7	8	9	10	11	12
Hay	21½	20½	19½	18½	17	16	15	14	13	12	11	10
Concentrate	5	6	7	8	9	10	11	12	13	14	15	16
Bran	1½	1½	1½	1½	2	2	2	2	2	2	2	2
Total lb	28	28	28	28	28	28	28	28	28	28	28	28
No. of feeds per day	3	3	3	3	4	4	4	4	4	4	4	4

NOTE:

a) Horses are highly individual, and no two rations will be exactly the same. The above chart is intended as a guide.

b) A horse of 15 hands will require less hay, and the concentrate ration can stop increasing at the 7 lb to 10 lb stage, unless the horse needs, and can take, more.

c) The smaller horse will start at 2 lb to 3 lb rather than 5 lb concentrate daily.

d) Big horses over 16 hands will require overall more food per day, and should be increased at about 1 lb per week extra. Let them have all the hay they will eat, provided they finish up their grain.

e) Concentrate includes grains — oats, maize, etc. and pellets (horse nuts). Watch the protein value of pelleted feed. If low protein is fed, increase quantity by one-third to give equivalent feed value.

Water

A constant supply of clean, fresh water must always be available to every horse in field and stable. Buckets must be refilled up to six times a day, and thoroughly scrubbed out twice a day. Without water no horse will thrive.

Routine

1. Regular routine is essential to the horse's well-being.
2. If it is summer when you are getting your horse fit, he may have been staying out all night until now. Now is the time to start bringing him in at night.
3. Exercise early — say from 5.30 or 6.0 a.m. — and on return from exercise give the horse his first feed.
4. After his feed turn him out for an hour or two until the flies get bad.
5. Bring him in about 10.0 a.m. and groom him.
6. Give midday feed and leave the horse to rest and digest.

7. If your schedule permits, return about 3.0 p.m., tack up and lunge for twenty minutes. (Lungeing may be done later, of course, if your schedule demands.)

8. After lungeing turn horse into the paddock again for a couple of hours.

9. Bring him in and feed him again about 7.0 p.m.

10. This routine will cut the grass intake considerably, and will enable the horse's body to tighten up and tune up.

Shoeing

Keep a careful eye on your horse's shoes. They will start to wear out about the fourth week. Most horses require shoeing every four to five weeks.

Fourth week

On the evening before a rest-day the horse should have a bran mash, and on rest-day the concentrate should be reduced by about half to avoid overheating. Whenever work is stopped for a day or two the concentrate ration should be reduced.

Exercise

1. The horse should now be working an hour and a half to two hours daily. Work should be split into road work, schooling and lungeing, preferably taking the horse out twice each day to achieve this total exercise time.

2. Road work should be steady and progressive, with trots now more frequent and longer.

3. Hills should be introduced now. Start by using gentle slopes, getting steeper as the days go by. Walk briskly up them at first, then start trotting up carefully. If horse starts blowing half-way up, let him walk.

4. By the end of the fourth week the horse should be able to trot up a reasonable slope if it is not too long.

5. Walking and trotting up hills builds the muscles of the hind-quarters and back. Strong hind-quarters are essential for speed and jumping.

6. Hill work also builds up the lungs and gives stamina.

7. When you are coming down hills take care to prevent the horse slipping. If the surface is good walk out down the hill as well as up it.

8. By the end of the fourth week the horse will be hardening up, and the muscles on his shoulders and quarters will be developing.

9. Even though the horse may feel fit and keen to go on, this is only the half-way mark. Do not risk his wind, heart and limbs by allowing him to over-exert himself.

Fitness of rider

It is no good having a fit horse and an unfit rider. If possible, the rider who is going to event or hunt the horse should be the one to get the horse fit.

To help the get-fit process use a skipping-rope fairly actively about ten minutes a day. This, combined with the riding, will ensure that you will be fit to ride your horse in competition, and will not flop about on him and cause a sore back.

Fifth week

1. If all has gone well during the first four weeks, and the horse has no sign of strain to its legs and is breathing freely and well, then you can allow a short, slow canter at the beginning of the fifth week.
2. Choose a field with really good going, free from holes and stones, and with plenty of give in the ground, without being slippery.
3. Walk the first half-mile or more, trot for a reasonable spell, walk again for several minutes, and then start trotting again in the field where you plan to canter. If the horse is settled and trotting well push him gently into a balanced canter. Avoid fuss, and do not let the horse 'explode' or rush off. Canter only a short distance and then ease back to trot and then walk.
4. Make all transitions smoothly, and avoid the risk of strain caused by sudden changes of pace. Keep rhythm in mind all the time.
5. Canter with the reins short and on contact, not loose, as this will encourage bucking. Even so, the horse may give a buck to express his enjoyment. Do not punish him much for this, but bring his head up and push him forward with the leg to discourage further bucking. Bucking can mean that the back muscles hurt and need stretching, or simply express enjoyment, but it is a habit which must be discouraged.

Diet and shoeing

1. Concentrate ration now up to 9 lb for 16 h.h. horse. The horse should now be fed four times a day. The time spent turned out to grass should be reduced to no more than three hours. If grass is plentiful, reduce the time even more.
2. The horse will now require re-shoeing. Toe clips in front and

quarter clips on the hind-shoe, with the toe of the shoe set back a little under the toe of the hoof, will stop the shoes from twisting in muddy going, and prevent the danger of overreaching.

3. Feather-edged hind-shoes — shoes with the inside edge of each shoe narrowed slightly so that they fit well under the wall — are essential to avoid interfering behind, now that faster work is starting.

4. Non-slip studs in the outside heel of the hind-shoes and both heels of the front shoes are necessary. They should be the screw-in variety, which can be changed for jumping studs, also screwed in, when the horse is schooling over fences.

General

1. By now the horse's coat should really shine, and move freely over hardening muscles. His flesh should be in the process of conversion into muscles which are beginning to bulge out above the fore-legs and on the quarters.

2. If the flesh is coming off rather than turning into muscle, or if the coat is staring, dull and dry, something is wrong. Either the horse has something wrong with it or you have not been feeding or grooming correctly. Call the vet and have the horse checked thoroughly — lungs, heart and, if he thinks it necessary, blood and urine too.

3. A horse can be both fit and big-bodied. Fit horses are hard and the body outline is trim, while the appearance is alert. A fat horse is soft; its stomach is well rounded and its appearance sleepy. A fit horse is not necessarily a lean horse — if the horse is lean he could need his teeth floating and/or to be de-wormed.

4. Poorness can also result from fretting or unhappiness. Try to discover the cause and correct the problem. A fit horse should be happy, with well-covered ribs, and its whole body should be moulded into a well-covered, hard shape.

5. By the end of the fifth week you should be doing two or three short canters per session without making the horse blow too hard. Also trot up plenty of long, gentle slopes. The horse should now be trotting on with long, ground-covering strides.

Sixth week

1. Providing all is going well, you can now start to let the horse out a little in canter. By the end of the week you should be able to enjoy a reasonable canter at medium speed, and the horse should require pulling up rather than coming to a walk on his own.

2. Pull up by reducing speed gently. Do not jerk the horse to a stop or to a slower speed. This causes injury.

Schooling

1. Work in sitting trot can now be started. Start with just a few minutes and work up gradually once the horse is happy and soft in his back. Sitting to the trot when it is uncomfortable to the rider is also uncomfortable to the horse, and serves no useful purpose.
2. After a few days start working sitting trot without stirrups to deepen and strengthen your seat.
3. Schooling should now become more serious and you can introduce 20 m and 15 m circles at sitting trot and 20 m circles at canter, as well as cantering on the long sides.
4. Do not overdo things, especially cantering circles. This is strenuous work even when the horse is properly fit, and it is important that the horse should always enjoy his schooling. If he is exhausted, or his muscles hurt from over-schooling when unfit, he will start to become resistant and stiff. The calmness and relaxation have then gone, and the work is valueless.

Grooming

1. Grooming, including strapping, will now take about a half-hour longer than the half- to three-quarters of an hour required so far. Do not skimp it; this strapping does pay dividends in muscle-formation.
2. If the rider is additionally the groom he or she will also get fitter by doing the strapping!

General

1. By the end of the sixth week small, light-framed horses will be at least three-quarters fit. They will have reached a stage when they can undertake moderately strenuous work for a short period of time.
2. Large horses with bigger frames will take another two weeks to reach a similar stage.

Seventh week

1. This is the start of the final phase of the getting-fit process. The seventh and eighth week are used as a build-up to real work.
2. It takes two weeks to tune up a fit horse for competition. Horses which you know can achieve real fitness in eight weeks can now

start their final preparation for competitions. With other horses, wait till the full eight weeks have elapsed and then add a two-week tune-up before competing.

3. Plan your competition programme carefully. Whether your horse is a novice or is experienced, do not over-enter during the early part of the season. One show or event every two weeks is really enough at the start, although it is possible to show once a week without damage. Give your horse time to recover from one competition before rushing it off to the next.

4. Travelling is tiring, especially if a horse is not used to it. Now is a good time to start bandaging and dressing him fully to travel and trailering a few miles away for your work or exercise.

5. Do not go far, and do drive with consideration for your horse. Let him learn how to balance himself in the trailer, so that he does not get exhausted when travelling to competitions.

8. Especially if you have been working alone, this is a good time to work your horse in company. Do not let the horses race each other when cantering, but you can speed the canters up a little, and even have a short half-speed gallop by the end of the week. Do not let your horse right out yet, and do not let him get unbalanced. Make sure that the footing you choose to gallop over is really good, sound going.

7. Another advantage of trailering away from home to work is to allow your horse to become accustomed to unloading and working amid strange surroundings with unusual sights and sounds. Some horses work very well at home but get over-excited and will not concentrate away from home, and this can be avoided with experience.

Schooling

1. Jumping can now be introduced into the daily work. Keep jumps few and small at first.

2. The objective is to get the horse going freely forward, and capable of absorbing the jar of landing. Do not make more than five or six small jumps on any one day during this week.

3. Jump a log or two when out exercising and three or four small fences in the paddock at home.

4. Over-jumping at this stage can induce strains which may cause the horse to be laid off and waste all your hours of slow work so far.

General

1. At this stage, even if the horse is nearly fit, he will probably warm up and sweat during his work. Up till now you should never have worked him to the point of sweating, even when he was completely soft.

2. This is the time to start your horse wearing a rug or blanket at night. If the weather is very warm use a sheet or light blanket, and put it on last thing. Otherwise use a regular night rug. You do not want the horse to be too warm, or to sweat under the blanket, but you must avoid the danger of chilling. The horse needs to be comfortable.

Eighth week

1. By now your horse should be very nearly fit and ready for hunting, sponsored rides, one-day eventing, showing, etc. Getting truly fit for racing or three-day eventing, which are activities requiring the horse to exert itself vigorously for quite a long period of time, will take two to four weeks more work.

2. The horse will now require between two and three hours' steady exercise each day.

3. On the second day of this week include a half-mile of gentle uphill slope in half-speed gallop, to see if your horse is breathing easily.

4. Most horses at this stage will sail on, and have to be restrained gently. If your horse tries to slow down, let him. He is not quite ready for the effort.

5. If he goes on well, gallop the half-mile, then slow to a canter, then back to a trot and then to a walk. Walk for a mile or two until the horse is cool. Once he is cool, cover another mile in trot, and finally walk the last mile home.

6. Always walk the last mile back to the stable to allow the horse to cool off.

7. This rule should only be broken in the event of heavy, cold rain, when walking would mean the horse getting chilled. In this case trot, so that he will come in warm and the rain will dry off him quicker.

Diet

1. The horse will now have reached the target of 12 lb concentrate for a 16 h.h. horse.

2. Horses going on into racing or three-day eventing will need to

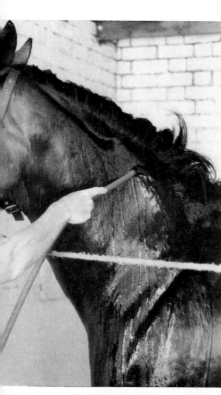

Plate XII. Bathing the horse.
A. Wet the horse thoroughly on one side with warm water.

B. Using a sponge, apply mild soap or equine shampoo and work up a lather, remembering chest, legs and under-side.

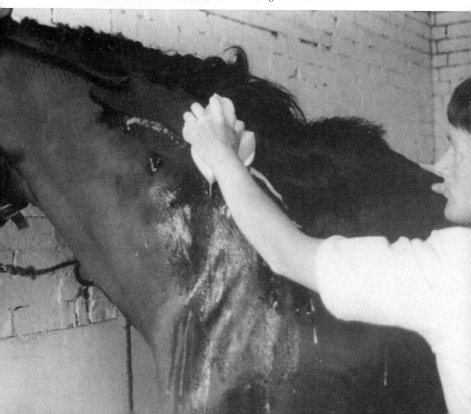

C. Rinse thoroughly with plenty of warm water, then remove surplus water with sweat-scraper.

D. Do not use sweat-scraper on legs below knees or hocks; in these areas use a large clean, damp sponge. Repeat the whole procedure on the other side of the horse.

E. Wet the tail thoroughly in a bucket of warm water.

F. Soap the tail, working from the bottom up to the top.

G. Rinse the tail thoroughly with plenty of warm water.

H. Swing or flip the tail to remove excess water, then 'comb' with your fingers to separate the hairs gently.

I. Wash the head and face with a damp sponge. Do not use soap on the head, and do not get water in the ears or eyes. Finish by rubbing the horse dry with a clean towel.

C

D

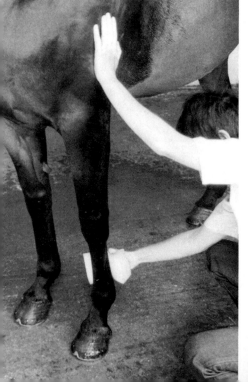

E

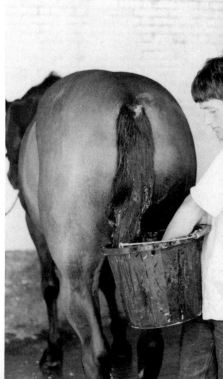

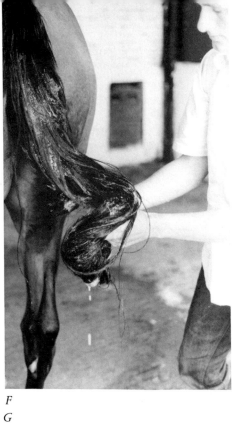

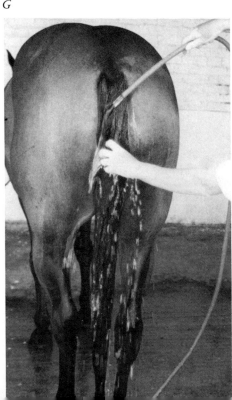
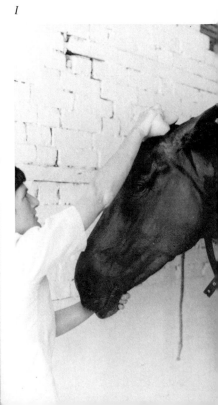

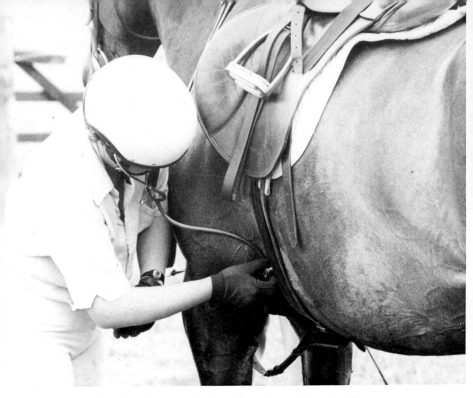

Plate XIII. *Taking the pulse and respiration with a stethoscope* (above) *and with the fingers under the jawbone* (below).

Plate XIV. A fit horse.

Plate XV. When you come out of the starting-box at the beginning of the cross-country have the horse attentive but not over-excited.

Plate XVI. A good, confident jump over an upright fence. The rider is perhaps a little far forward, but does not appear to have approached too fast, and is looking up and ahead.

Plate XVII.   A

B

Plate XVII. Two trakehner fences.
A. A less experienced but still confident horse and rider clear the fence well. The rider should be looking up and forward (see opposite*).*

B. This combination appears very confident, and is jumping well. The rider is slightly left behind, but is very secure, and has left the horse's head free.

A

Plate XVIII. *Two examples of a spread fence. A. The horse took off a little soon and left the rider slightly behind; nevertheless, both horse and rider are making a good, confident jump. B. A very. confident, experienced horse. Take-off was exactly right, and the rider is in a good position. The rider could improve by relaxing the elbows to the sides and allowing the toes to point to the front.*

B

increase this intake over the next two to four weeks to between 14 lb and 16 lb, depending on the size and temperament of the individual.

3. Remember that all horses are individuals, and will have to be fed with knowledge and understanding of their individuality. Some horses may be happy and equally fit on less than 12 lb a day, but 12 lb is certainly sufficient for a 16 h.h. horse.

General

1. Check your horse's legs for coolness each night and morning. Any sign of slight heat can be your early-warning signal of something wrong.
2. The third day of the eighth week should be a normal work-out that does not call for too much strain on the legs, and on the fourth day repeat the gallop and work as on the second day.
3. If your horse is entered in a competition on the sixth day he should now be ready to run. The fifth day would be a normal, not too stressful, exercise day. The seventh day, of course, will be his rest-day.
4. If you have entered a one-day event do not be over-ambitious your first time out. Ride your dressage and jumping phases. Before going on cross-country check your horse's legs for coolness very thoroughly. Do not go on cross-country if there is even slight heat anywhere. Better to save the horse for the next competition.
5. If all is well with his legs, ride the cross-country with consideration for your horse. Do not worry about time faults. Allow the horse to stay well within himself.
6. Bad falls are often caused by asking too much of your horse before he is ready. Better to take it slowly and have a horse to ride in the next competition.
7. If you have been getting fit for hunting remember that the first few days should be only half-days — no more than a couple of hours. Hunting requires a very fit horse.
8. Always put the welfare of your horse before your own pleasure and you will not go wrong.

Shoeing

By the end of the eighth week your horse will need to be reshod. This time fit shoes suitable for the work your horse will be doing. If he is eventing he will require stud-holes for the screw-in jumping studs.

Exercise and work

1. Getting a horse really fit is a long, slow process and requires lots of hard work. Once your horse is fit for the work you require of him, it is important to keep him so.

2. Exercise consists of giving the horse enough walking and trotting to keep his muscles toned up and to prevent him getting over-exuberant, but without tiring him or subjecting his legs to undue stress.

3. Work is when the horse is ridden for the pleasure of the rider and is taken out for a 'good ride'. A 'good ride' would include canters, a slow gallop, maybe some cross-country jumping. The horse and rider may get muddy and tired, but will have had a good time. Hunting, hunter trials, eventing, show-jumping, showing, polo, racing, sponsored trail riding are all labelled work. Work calls for stress and strain, and should not be done every day.

4. On days when a horse is not required to 'work' in the above sense he must be properly exercised.

5. This exercise can be achieved by the horse being ridden out by a competent rider, or led beside a ridden horse (wearing a blanket if he is clipped and the weather is cold), or being lunged.

6. If nothing else is possible, turn the horse out for an hour or so to exercise himself. If the weather is cold he should wear a New Zealand rug; if it is warm he will not need a rug.

7. Once a horse is fit he should not be turned out to graze for more than an hour a day. If he is being hand-walked to graze for twenty minutes or so he will not need to be turned out at all. Some grazing will relax the horse, and help to prevent boredom. Too much grass will take up room in the stomach that is required for hard food.

8. The amount of exercise required by a fit horse once he is working depends on the amount of work being done. The day after hard work he only needs to stretch his legs for a while. On other days he will need one and a half to two hours of exercise.

9. If no fast work has been done for a week or so the horse will require a long exercise of about three hours or fifteen miles.

10. The horse is being fed for hard work, and it is better to exercise him properly if there is a gap in his work programme than to cut his feed once he is fit.

11. Especially if someone else is exercising the horse, plan your routes, know how long they take at a given pace (or combination

of paces) and work out your routine according to how much exercise your horse requires on a given day.

General

1. Stable routine plays a large part in the care of fit horses. Horses thrive best on a fixed schedule. Start early in the morning — 6 a.m. or 6.30 a.m. is good practice. This allows plenty of time to fit in the four feeds necessary for the fit horse, and also ensures that a sick horse is found early and action is taken. Time is often vital if a horse is really sick, and all stables are going to have trouble some time.
2. Cleanliness is essential to health. If you want to keep your horse fit it is worth taking the trouble to know how everything should be done thoroughly and correctly, and setting yourself and your staff high standards.
3. Carelessness leads to injury and sickness, and can spoil all your hours of hard work getting your horse fit.
4. Clean stables with clean floors swept or raked each morning and plenty of clean bedding put down are essential.
5. The horse should have plenty of fresh water in a clean bucket always available.
6. The best-quality food, well prepared in clean buckets and given in a clean manger, is vital.
7. Adequate, steady exercise, thorough daily grooming with a clean grooming kit, regular worming every six to eight weeks, regular shoeing every four to five weeks with shoes which are the correct weight and fit for the horse and the work being done, and kind, firm handling will keep your horse happy, healthy and fit.

Interval training

Definition

Interval training is a method whereby the heart, lungs and muscles are stressed, then rested a short while and allowed to recover partially, then stressed again. This builds increased tolerance to stress, and can be carefully regulated by built-in checks.

Physiology of sustained exertion

1. Given time, animal physique adapts itself to the demands made upon it.

2. One of the waste products of energy-production is lactic acid. An unconditioned physique is limited in the amount of effort it can sustain by the ability of the circulatory system to remove this lactic acid from the muscles.

3. If body systems are unfit for the demands made on them, lactic acid cannot be removed from the muscle fibres quickly enough. It builds up, and the muscles become tired, ache and lose their elasticity. If they are not allowed to rest, serious injury may result.

4. This form of fatigue causes bowed tendons or pulled muscles, and if the horse is forced to continue, possible crashing falls.

5. If the horse is fit, sufficient oxygen is available in the bloodstream for the muscles to go on working, reoxidizing lactic acid back to glycogen for more energy-production.

6. Interval training, by exposing the body to limited stress alternated with rest, improves respiration and circulation. This gradually creates a demand for more oxygen, and the muscles become capable of sustained effort without undue fatigue.

Application
The system can be applied two ways:
1. To develop speed.
2. To increase stamina, in order to make it possible to maintain speed for a longer distance.

Preparation
1. Before trying interval training on your horse, try it yourself. It will help you to get very fit, and will give you an understanding of the critical, exacting process of training.

2. Wrongly applied — especially to a 'dumb' animal — interval training could be dangerous to health.

3. Use a 400m track, or at least a measured distance of 400 metres.

4. To develop speed, sprint 100 metres, then complete the lap by walking or jogging the remaining 300. Repeat four times, or until you are too winded to continue. Some top athletes can make ten repetitions.

5. To increase stamina, run a full lap, 400 metres, at about ten miles per hour (a little over 250 metres per minute). This means completing the lap in about 1 min 35.5 sec. Then walk one lap, 400 metres, for a rest interval. Repeat four times, or as many times as you are able. Again, top athletes could probably make as many as ten repetitions.

You should be in good physical shape before starting to practise interval training. You will certainly be impressed by the results you can obtain, and having tried it yourself you will be much more careful not to overdo it with your horse.

Interval training for horses

Horses must be given a good foundation of long, slow work before starting with interval training. If you have followed the system I have laid out for getting your horse fit you could use interval training in trot from about the fourth week. *Never practise Interval Training more than twice a week.*

Principles of conditioning

1. The object is to develop more resistance to fatigue by increasing the efficiency of the respiratory and cardio-vascular systems.
2. Interval training accomplishes this by stressing the muscular system, and then allowing partial recovery during an interval of walking or jogging, and then repeating the stress interval.
3. Because the horse cannot tell you in words how he feels you have to learn to read the signs of discomfort and stress he demonstrates under exercise.
4. Physical exertion uses energy. Energy is supplied to the muscles by blood. Exercise always produces increased activity of the heart and lungs, which continues for a period of time after the exercise ceases, until the energy previously stored in the muscles has been replaced. Then the heart and lung action returns to normal.
5. Normal action may vary slightly from horse to horse.
6. In addition to the heart and lungs, body temperature is an indication of the horse's general state of health, and rises with exercise.
7. The expression TPR, used in interval training, stands for Temperature, Pulse and Respiration. These are the three vital signs which can be monitored to tell you of the horse's state of health or fitness at any given moment.
8. At the compulsory ten-minute check before the cross-country, Phase D in a three-day event, the vet takes the TPR of each horse in order to decide whether or not it is fit to continue.

TPR — how to take it and how to use it

1. Normal temperature for a horse is 100°F (nearly 38°C), plus or

minus 1 degree subject to the age of the horse, the time of day taken.

2. Normal pulse, at rest, is 36–44 beats per minute.

3. Normal respiration, at rest, is 12–15 breaths per minute.

4. To take pulse, gently place the fingers under the jawbone on either side, or use a stethoscope on the left side just behind the elbow. Take a fifteen-second count and multiply by four. (It may be necessary to take a count of a full minute to catch any abnormalities of the pulse.)

5. To take respiration, watch the horse's flank. Count only 'one' for each breath — that is, count only in. Again, using the second hand on your watch, count for fifteen seconds and multiply by four.

6. Neither pulse nor respiration should ever be allowed to exceed the safety limit of 100 during work, although they may go up quite high. What matters is how quickly they return to normal.

7. Pulse and respiration should return to normal in 15 to 20 minutes. For either to take longer indicates excessive stress — or possibly sickness.

8. It is not necessary to wait 20 to 30 minutes for full recovery of P and R to measure the stress factor. If you take a reading in 5 minutes the horse should be one-sixth recovered, in 10 minutes he should be one-third recovered and in 15 minutes he should be half recovered — if we take 30 minutes as a base.

9. Interval training allows you to develop your own programme (making use of the ground available) by selecting distances, pace, gait and times according to your particular needs, and repeating the intervals until optimum stress is reached.

10. The possibilities are almost unlimited. You, as the trainer, keep a watchful eye on the P and R. As the horse gets fit you may want to increase pace, distance, or time. Or you may change to more demanding terrain. Much will depend upon your judgment, and the type of event for which you are preparing.

11. When the horse is fit the pulse rate will stabilize. If your horse while at rest has a pulse rate of 30 or less you may be sure you have an outstanding athlete.

12. Respiration count will vary more with the day-to-day temperature than pulse-rate, because more rapid breathing is necessary to reduce body heat. In hot weather respiration will increase more than pulse-rate. Since pulse-rate is more stable, it is a more reliable gauge of condition.

13. When beginning interval training with your horse start with only two sets of repetitions of your interval of stress and your interval of rest. This should produce NO apparent stress. If it does the work is too strenuous and must be reduced either by lessening the pace of the stress interval, or diminishing the time of the stress interval, or changing the gait or using easier terrain.

14. Stress should be built up gradually by repeating the sets of intervals. A sequence of five intervals should always be the maximum number.

How to use interval training

1. You must be able to control the programme by knowing how far and how fast you are going. Find a large field or track with good footing and mark off 1,600 metres (1 mile), in 400-metre segments. If you do not have room for this just mark off 400 metres (a quarter of a mile).

2. Cover the 400 m at trot in 1 min 49 sec, which is a speed of 220 mpm, the required pace for phases A and C, roads and tracks in a three-day event.

3. It may take several tries to get the timing accurate. An average, untrained horse trots at about 200 mpm, so it may take your horse nearly two minutes to cover the 400 m the first time you try. Rest your horse with two or three minutes of walk between each try, but persevere until you get it right.

4. If you are only in week 4 or 5 of the fitting programme leave the exercise after you get the right speed if you took more than two repetitions to do so. If not, complete two repetitions and then leave interval training until the 5th or 6th week.

5. When you next practise interval training, in the 5th or 6th week, trot 400 metres in 1 min 49 sec (or as close as you can to it), then walk 3 minutes and repeat the trot sequence. Dismount and check the P and R — if well under the stress levels, repeat the intervals twice more. Dismount, check P and R, walk 10 minutes in hand and check P and R again. By this time they should have returned to normal. Note all figures in your notebook as you go along.

6. To achieve worth-while results with interval training it is important to keep a notebook with an accurate record of the statistics each time you do interval work.

7. Note weather conditions, including temperature and humidity.

8. Record the length of interval used — e.g. 400 metres — the pace

used (e.g. 220 mpm), the length of the rest interval (e.g. 3 minutes) at walk, and the number of repetitions.

9. Note the P and R at rest before leaving the stable — it will be between 32 and 44 beats per minute.

10. Warm up in walk, trot and slow canter and then check P and R. The pulse may be about 65 beats per minute, which is your horse's normal 'warmed-up' level.

11. This practice at the trot will get you started on interval training with your horse, and give you practice at taking P and R. The real work is done at canter, or slow gallop, and should not begin until your horse has had his eight weeks of basic conditioning.

More advanced application

1. Once in the 8th week of conditioning, interval training at canter may start.

2. Using the same measured 400 metres, after at least half an hour of warm-up in walk and trot, canter the distance in 1 min 4 sec — a speed of 350 mpm.

3. Walk for 3 minutes and repeat. Check P and R — if they are well under the stress limits repeat the intervals twice more. Dismount, check P and R, hand-walk for 10 minutes and check P and R again. If the horse is back to his normal (warmed-up) pulse and respiration rate you may continue to the next level. If not, stay at this level until he does recover in the 10 minutes.

4. The next step is to increase the time spent at canter from 1 min 4 sec to 3 minutes. Depending on the individual horse, you may wish to use a speed of 400 mpm for this work. If the horse is fairly big and long-striding he will be more comfortable cantering at 400, or even 425, mpm. This means covering the 400-metre distance in 1 minute (400 mpm) or 57 sec (approx 425).

5. Canter 3 minutes at 400 mpm (1,200 metres), walk 3 minutes, repeat intervals twice more. Dismount and check P and R. Hand-walk for ten minutes and check P and R. If the horse returns to normal in 10 minutes increase repetitions up to 5 times.

6. A horse capable of returning to normal in 10 minutes after five repetitions of 3-minute canter stints at 400 mpm can easily cope with a pre-training-level event.

7. The amount of effort required from the horse is mainly determined by the speed and the distance. Apart from the number of repetitions, these are the factors normally varied.

8. Short distances at high speeds develop strength and speed — e.g., ¾ or full-speed gallops for 500 metres.
9. Longer, slower gallops develop strength and the rhythm of a horse's stride, which is conducive to staying power — e.g., half-speed gallops for 700 metres.

Preparation for three-day events

1. In working out more advanced systems of interval training various formulae are used. The factors are generally expressed:

   D — Distance of each effort.

   V — Speed of each effort.

   I — Interval, or time allowed for partial recovery between efforts.

   A — Activity (walk or trot) during recovery period.

   R — Repetition of consecutive efforts with intervals between.

2. If D.R.I. and A are kept constant, and V is progressively increased, you will develop mainly speed.
3. As the horse adapts himself to the speed required over a given distance, the number of repetitions can be progressively increased to develop stamina at that speed.
4. You would then keep the factors D.V.I.A. constant and R variable.
5. More traditional systems of fitting vary only the speed and distance. Long, slow canters supplemented with short, sharp gallops later in the conditioning programme. Usually there are no repetitions on the same day, so the horse's oxygen-level is allowed to return to normal after one extended exertion.
6. Using interval training and keeping D.R.I.A. constant, V variable, you can work up to the speed required over a period of 6 or 7 weeks.
7. During the last 6 weeks before a three-day event you keep D.V.I.A. constant with R variable, thus preparing the horse to go the required distance at that speed.
8. Distance should be kept down to 600 metres (less than half a mile), but repetitions are gradually increased up to six or more.
9. *Interval training must not be done more than twice a week.* The other days are used for slow work over varied ground, and for jumping and dressage.

10. Interval training is not an 'easy alternative' to more traditional methods. It involves formulae, time calculations, heart-rates, respiration rates, etc. But it is simpler in practice than it appears in writing, and it has already led to undreamed-of improvements with human athletes, and is daily being more studied and used by horsemen.

Words of caution

1. Dismount IMMEDIATELY after completing your gallops and take pulse and respiration and record the figure. (In most horses the ratio of pulse to respiration is 4 to 1, and this ratio should remain the same when stressed.)
2. Walk in hand 10 minutes and take P and R again. Record this figure, then cool out the horse. Compare these figures with the figures from the next work. Be alert to changes.
3. Regardless of a slower pulse-rate, when respiration approaches 100 it is time to stop work and cool out. Clock the time it takes for P and R to return to normal. If it is too long, reduce work-load.
4. The total of pulse and respiration should NEVER exceed 180. If it does the horse is exhausted. The total should drop 30 per cent within 10 minutes.
5. If the pulse exceeds 100, and has not dropped at least 20 per cent within 10 minutes, the horse is exhausted. The work-load must be reduced. The same applies to respiration.
6. If respiration exceeds pulse the horse is exhausted.
7. The horse's maximum effective pulse-rate is about 120. To achieve improvement in your horse's capacity he should be stressed sufficiently to raise his pulse 60 per cent of maximum (i.e., to 72 beats per minute).
8. Stay alert for signs of stress while riding — e.g., gasping for breath, blowing, stumbling and slowing the pace. If they appear, do not finish the work-out; pull up gently, dismount and walk your horse.
9. It is important for your horse to be relaxed as he works. Tension and stiffness are tiring. A relaxed, contented horse will often snort (or sneeze), will flex obediently, and will be receptive to your aids.
10. For the novice trainer, or one new to interval training, I recommend increasing the distance slightly once your horse handles the work-load easily rather than increasing the speed.

Distance can be increased from 400 metres to 600 metres, and later to 800 metres (half a mile), or you can use a more hilly terrain to stress the horse more. Too much speed can bring your horse to his peak condition too soon. After reaching his peak he will 'go stale' — i.e., his condition will take a downward turn.

Over-training

1. Ideally, your horse should reach peak condition on the day of the event. If he starts to drop off return to long, slow work. Perhaps your entire programme contains too much speed: this will bring your horse to his peak too quickly, and he will trail off more rapidly.
2. A horse maintains peak condition longer when he is brought up slowly, and the drop-off is more gradual.
3. A properly trained horse will still be quite fit after a drastic reduction in his work-load, and will stay fit for some time.
4. It is easier to over-train than to under-train. Let your horse rest after a hard work-out or a competition. A horse in need of rest will become irritable, just like a person.
5. Keep your horse happy. A HAPPY horse is more resistant to fatigue. Be considerate and kind to him; don't nag. Treat him like a winner and he will become a winner.

PART THREE
The speed and endurance test

The cross-country

Purpose

The course-designer's objective is to test the horse's speed, endurance and jumping ability and the rider's ability to control and use the horse properly.

Each level asks different things. The lower levels are introductory and educational. The Intermediate and Advanced levels test the well-prepared horse and rider.

Basic problems

At all levels the same basic problems are encountered. The obstacles pose questions:

1. Is the horse in balance, and can the rider get him to the fence? The rider must know, and be able to produce, the correct length of frame; he must evaluate the approach for speed and positioning.
2. Is the horse responsive? Does he shorten, lengthen, turn, speed up or slow down as desired, remaining in balance and with sufficient impulsion to negotiate the fence?
3. In a series of obstacles, does the rider have the horse between his hands and legs so that he is on the right line, jumping at the right point and desired speed?

Seven basic obstacles

In all events there are seven basic types of obstacles. These vary in size and difficulty according to the level of competition.

1. Straightforward uprights.
2. Spreads.
3. Obstacles without height — ditches, water, etc.
4. Banks.
5. Drops.
6. Water — jumps into water, jumps positioned in water, jumps out of water.
7. Brush or bullfinch fences.

Classic problems

The course-designer sets out to test the horse and rider in four basic areas:

1. Distance.
2. Turning.
3. Banks.
4. Controlled boldness.

Types and combinations of fences used to test these abilities are:

1. *Distance*

   The classic distance problem is the road crossing. The rider must find the line, get the horse to adjust speed and length of stride to make the distance correctly. For example, he may have to take one or both fences at an angle to get extra space or the correct distance. The best way through is always the straight line if at all possible, rather than sudden sharp changes of direction. Distance problems are becoming much more complex at higher levels, and may include jumping corners and double bounces, with probably a choice of line.

2. *Turning*

   A typical turning problem is presented by a pen. The rider must find the line, jump in, turn 90° and jump out. At highest levels this may involve a variety of fences and a number of different options. This demands a responsive horse, to slow down and make the turn and yet not lose impulsion or waste time.

3. *Banks*

   Banks and drops ask the horse to remain in balance while levels of take-off and landing are changing. At lower levels this may be a

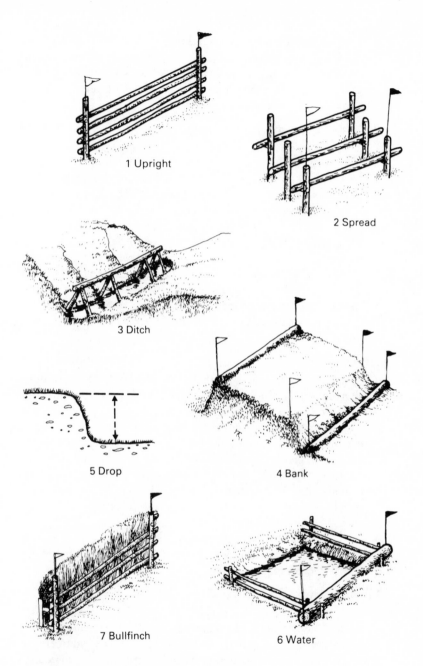

Diagram 19. Seven basic obstacles

simple step up or down. At Preliminary and Intermediate levels the horse may be asked to jump on to a table-top and down, or down into a sunken area and up. At Advanced level the question may include other problems — for example, up on to a bank, a distance problem, and then a drop.

4. *Controlled boldness*

Boldness is tested throughout the course, and a good course will never penalize a horse who jumps boldly. To jump off in water, to jump through brush, to jump into water, all require boldness. The classic test of controlled boldness would be a coffin. This is a series of fences, first a vertical down a short, steep slope, then a ditch, then an uphill slope and a vertical: three jumping efforts with changes of terrain. Boldness is tested by asking the horse to jump down into something when he probably cannot see the bottom. The horse must be controlled, because if he is going too fast he may run down the slope and fall into the ditch, or run into the far rails after jumping the ditch.

Other tests for controlled boldness are, for example, a series of downhill fences set at angles.

Course evaluation

1. A well-designed course will help the rider to develop a smooth rhythm on the course. Problem fences will be spaced out, and between them will be breather fences.
2. The most difficult fences should be in the middle third of the course. At the beginning the horse will not be prepared, and by the end he may be tired, and very difficult fences may cause a fall.
3. At lower levels the object is basically to show the horse the different kinds of obstacles. Forty to 50 per cent of the horses should go clear across country. Only about 10 to 15 per cent should be eliminated.
4. At higher levels, particularly three-day events, a quarter to a third should go clear, and a quarter to a third should be eliminated on cross-country.

One-day events and horse trials

1. The speed and endurance phase will probably consist of cross-country course only. No roads and tracks, no steeplechase.
2. Some one-day events may have a very short roads and tracks. If so, it acts as a warm-up, and is useful preparation for three-day eventing.

Walking the course

1. Walking the cross-country course is very important, not only for becoming familiar with the terrain but also for making decisions about the approach to multiple obstacles and alternate fences.

2. Walk the course at least three times, preferably four.

3. The first walk gives you an overall impression of the fences and the terrain, and also your very important 'first impression' of each fence. This is the way the horse will see the course when you ride it. He won't know that the apparently innocent hedge hides a big ditch, or that the apparent confusion of posts and rails is actually a simple in-and-out.

4. As you walk, think all the time about what your horse's reaction will be.

5. About 40 metres from each fence, stop and take a good look at it. Then walk slowly forward towards it, paying attention to how the jump takes shape.

6. Appearances are often deceptive, and horses often react wrongly, therefore it is important for the rider to think what his or her horse's reaction will be, and to be prepared to modify the approach accordingly.

7. Always check the number on each fence as you walk round; it is easy to miss a fence. After every few fences stop and think back to make sure you have memorized the course and fences so far.

8. Look at the ground on the take-off and landing sides of the fence, and notice whether it is likely to become deep or boggy after the first dozen or so horses have gone, or whether it is well drained and will hold up well.

9. Pay attention to the going between fences too. Some courses are consistent all the way round, and others go from hard to soft, from level to rough. All variations make a difference to your speed and how your horse will cope with the course.

10. Whenever the course goes through wooded land look for hidden stumps, roots or low, overhanging branches. Also notice particularly jumps which are INTO the woods, where you may be jumping from bright sunshine into deep shade.

11. Combinations of fences and alternate fences demand careful consideration of all the possibilities. Pay particular attention to the flagging, numbering and penalty zones. Do not make any final decisions about your line through on this first walk; just get your first impression into your mind.

12. Always check the depth of any water jumps and the footing

under the water. Do this by walking into the water and feeling the bottom for yourself. Sometimes the water will be much deeper at one side of the fence than at the other, or there may be a hole in the bottom at one spot which you can avoid if you know about it beforehand.

13. If you are drawn late in the day consider how the position of the sun may affect the fences at the time you ride, and also how the going may have been altered by all the horses which have gone before you. Think about how the fences may be changed, too, by the presence of crowds around them.

14. If at all possible, make your second walk around the course in reverse order — that is, start with the last fence and walk back towards the first. This will give you the opportunity to study the landing side of each fence, and also to ensure that you take the best line from fence to fence, regardless of where the organizers place the directional markers.

15. After walking the course once forward and once backward sit down with the course plan provided by the organizers and consider the course as a whole. You have studied each fence individually, but you must now consider them in relation to each other. This will help in determining the appropriate speed, and perhaps avoid getting going too fast over a series of fairly straightforward fences, which may lead to carelessness. Consider also the terrain — is it steeply up and down hill, or relatively flat; is it twisty and trappy, or straightforward and rolling? Steep hills and a roundabout route will tire your horse quickly. Finally, consider the weather conditions. Hot, humid conditions will take a lot out of your horse, perhaps even more than icy winds and cold rain. Rain will affect the going, too. If the ground is baked and dry and then it rains just a little the going may be very slippery, especially on certain turns or at certain fences.

16. Now set out on your third cross-country walk. This time you should be checking your intended route and deciding exactly how far to the right or left of each marker you will pass. Keep a constant check on your approaches, and find yourself landmarks all the way round to enable you to take the shortest and quickest route towards, over and away from each fence. The landmarks should be permanent and clearly visible — for example, telephone poles, pylons, buildings or even trees (as long as you are sure you can recognize them again). At the World

Championships in Lexington, Kentucky in 1978 the sixth and seventh fences were two walls, not directly opposite each other but slightly offset, and forming a road crossing. The easiest and most direct route through was a diagonal line which was itself straight, but which meant jumping both the walls at a slight angle. Surprisingly few people had stood back and thus been enabled to see this relatively easy line through the combination, and I watched rider after rider jump the first wall, almost stop, make a sharp left turn, then a sharp right turn and then jump the second element. Stopping, starting and sharp turns all 'take the stuffing' out of your horse, and should be avoided on cross-country if possible.

17. If it is practicable, make this third walk around the course at the time of day you will have to ride it. The position of the sun can make a great difference to the appearance of a fence. Consider also the difference which will be made to fences once they are surrounded by a crowd of people. Whenever possible choose a line through a fence or combination which gives an obvious route away on landing, possibly between lines of spectators or down a path between the trees. Choosing a route where the horse must apparently jump straight into the crowd can cause him to drop his hind-legs too soon, or even hesitate on take-off.

18. You should set out on this third walk knowing what lies ahead, and particularly having taken note of any difficult landings, or big drop fences where jumping on one side may give your horse a much easier landing and departure than jumping on the other. Your aim is to go round quickly, saving every possible second, but a refusal or a fall will usually banish all hope of a prize, so your pace and your route must also be prudent. As you ride the cross-country remain sensitive to your horse, and how tired he is getting. Always keep in mind the last few jumps — you MUST have enough horse left to clear them.

19. This walk round is when you make your final decision on your first choice of route. Remember that the horse's experience over one fence will affect the way he jumps the next. Big drops will jar his legs and back, and will make him more cautious at the next drop fence. Sometimes there is no way to avoid the big drop, but if there is — and especially if you know that there is another drop coming which cannot be avoided — then it may pay to give the horse the easiest route, even at the expense of a second or two.

20. One jumping effort takes less out of your horse than two, and is usually quicker, provided it takes a direct route, towards the next fence.

21. Walk all alternatives carefully. Once you have decided on your first choice of route, decide on your second and third choice. Corners can save time and jumping efforts but they are tests of obedience, and must be ridden accurately, to the INCH. Since corners always involve a considerable spread they will require impulsion and absolute accuracy. They are best avoided with a tired horse or at the end of a long course. If you do decide on a corner, pick out a good landmark to give you an exact line.

22. Provided your horse has been properly trained to maintain the straight line on which he is put, you may want to angle certain elements in the interests of taking the shortest, most direct route. Remember that angling obstacles requires accuracy and obedience, and with wide parallels it should not be attempted. Hitting a fence when jumping diagonally is very likely to cause a fall. Jumping diagonally on to slopes or into water is risky, and jumping diagonally through bullfinch fences should not be attempted, since on the diagonal the brush will appear impenetrable to the horse. A tired horse finds it easier to jump straight over fences than to angle them, so towards the end of the course angling fences is best avoided.

23. Make absolutely certain that you know and understand the rules governing the particular event in which you are riding with regard to the numbering of elements of the same obstacle or fences which are very close together. If you do have a refusal you must be absolutely certain whether you should attempt only the element at which you refused or whether you must, or you may, re-jump any other elements. The rules do vary between one-day events and three-day events, and depending on the numbering of the obstacles. Work out now exactly what course you will follow if you do have a refusal at any element in any combination. Discovering and investigating all the alternatives and deciding exactly how you will proceed in the case of an unexpected refusal will save valuable seconds and help to avoid your becoming flustered and confused on course.

24. During this walk (and probably the previous one), it is helpful to walk with your trainer, or a knowledgeable friend, with whom you can discuss the problems and possibilities at each fence.

25. The final walk — which is the exact walking of the track you

intend to follow — should be done alone, and if possible at a time when there are few people around to distract you or obstruct your clear view. Early morning or late evening are usually good times. You should feel that the route you have chosen will enable you to achieve a good rhythm and consistent speed (although obviously there will be parts of the course where you have to slow down, and other places where you can gallop on).

26. Remember that your goal is to jump each obstacle with the minimum effort and to take the shortest possible route. Avoid unnecessary checking and shortening of the horse's stride, which along with sharp turns and sudden increases of pace will tire him quickly, and can cause leg problems. To win you must jump the fences without penalty. Speed is certainly a consideration, but avoidance of any waste of time in jumping the obstacles may be even more crucial than speed on the flat, so thorough, careful preparation and course walking is essential.

Riding the course

1. *The starting-box and the first fence*

   a) If you are competing in a one-day event or horse trial you will need to mount up and warm up a bit for cross-country. Check that the event is running on time (or if late, how much time you have before you start), and get mounted twenty to thirty minutes ahead of that.

   b) You will have ridden your dressage test earlier in the day, so now walk the horse for ten minutes to loosen him up again, have a canter for two or three minutes as a 'pipe-opener', and then jump the practice fences three or four times each. Start out with a trot fence over a small X (two rails crossed like an X) two or three times, then a small vertical in trot, and finally canter over a vertical and a small spread two or three times.

   c) If your horse has been properly schooled and prepared all you have to do is loosen him up — this is no place to train him.

   d) With two minutes to go to your starting-time, walk vigorously around near the starting-box. Make sure the starter knows you are close by at least five minutes ahead. Do not enter the box until the last possible moment before the start — i.e., when the starter says 20 seconds to go. Until you enter the box, keep moving. You can trot gently and make halt transitions or just keep walking, but do not stand still.

e) Have a trainer or knowledgeable friend close by you at the start in case you need any help with equipment or your horse gives you a problem entering the box. You are just about to embark on the most exciting part of the day, but try to remain calm, and your horse will be much more relaxed.

f) If you are riding in a three-day event you will have spent the previous ten minutes in the vet-box, and your preparations for the start of cross-country will be slightly different. This is covered in the section entitled 'What to do in the Vet-box.'

g) Once in the starting-box the horse should be brought to a halt, facing the exit on a straight line towards the first fence. Shorten your reins and get yourself ready to kick the minute the starter says 'Go'. You do need to be keyed up, and attentive, but do not get over-excited or you risk leaving the box too soon and having a 'false start', which is taken out of your time for cross-country and should be avoided.

h) Do not try to come out of the starting-box like a bullet out of a gun. However, you do want to establish a good rhythm and have the horse strongly between your legs and hands before you arrive at the first fence.

i) You will not be going at the pace you will pick up for the rest of the round until you have jumped maybe two or three fences, but you should be going determinedly forward, and straight towards your first fence.

j) Course-designers usually try to make the first fence fairly inviting, but even so most novices find it the hardest fence on the course. You are usually asking your horse to go AWAY from other horses, you have not really got into the swing of the course, and you will need more determination and more impulsion to jump the first fence well than any other fence on the course.

k) If you feel your horse is a bit sticky, use your whip three or four strides away from the fence, then put both hands back on the reins and ride hard with seat, legs and hands. It is better to over-ride the first fence than to have a refusal, and most novice riders do not realize how important it is to have the horse moving forward strongly into the hand. He can then be steadied, and collected as necessary for the next fence, but if he isn't there, on the bit, you have nothing to collect.

l) As with all fences (but particularly at the first fence), try to approach straight for the centre, jump fluently and with lots of impulsion, and move away from the fence accelerating somewhat. This will help your horse to realize that you mean business, and will get his concentration on the job in hand.

m) The siting of the first fence can definitely either help you or hinder you. Make sure you have thought about it from the point of view of your horse, and if possible watch some other competitors start out, so that you can see how the fence rides and possibly learn from their mistakes.

2. *Upright or vertical fences*

a) Most upright or vertical fences have an 'airy' look, and horses often do not respect them and want to take them too fast. It is usually a good plan to check the horse back about ten strides away and then ride the fence very balanced, a little more like show-jumping.

b) Time lost by doing this can be made up somewhere else on the course, and coming in too fast at upright timber can easily cause a fall.

c) Trakehner fences — where the ground drops away from a single rail — should be ridden much like upright timber, but more strongly. If the horse is bold there are no problems, but a less bold horse may have to be driven up harder into your hand, checked, and then the stride increased towards the fence. Do not run the horse on from ten strides away because there is a danger of running into the bottom of the fence, but rather balance him at ten strides away, drive him up into your hand and hold him until you see your stride at four strides out, and then ride on, increasing the stride.

d) Do not try to adjust speed or length of stride when you are closer to the fence than four strides away. By then it is too late, and you will only confuse your horse.

e) Although you should carry a whip cross-country (and, of course, use it if you feel the need to increase your speed, or impulsion), it is often more effective to use your seat, legs and spurs when within three or four strides of a fence. This avoids taking a hand off the reins at a time when you particularly need a good contact, and also weakening your position and possibly upsetting the balance of the horse.

f) With an upright fence preceded by a ditch, even though the ditch forms a kind of ground-line for the fence, horses have a tendency to be set back a little by the ditch. Again, check at about ten strides out and ride the horse strongly into your hand, engaging his hind-quarters so that his engine is right underneath him and can act effectively. Then try to ride as close to the ditch as possible. Do not gallop on strung out at a fence which is preceded by a ditch, particularly a vertical, as the horse may be inclined to take off too soon and flatten.

g) With all fences you should see the exact spot you plan to jump, and ride right to it. This is even more important with upright fences than, say, with ascending oxers, which tend to be much easier for the horse to see and respect. If you cannot tell when you are four strides away exactly, and ride on from there, at least check the horse and balance him well when you are about ten strides away. Then hold him between your legs and your hand, balanced, straight and impulsive. It will then be much easier for him to deal with an awkward distance than if he is strung out, and perhaps unbalanced.

h) Upright fences followed by a drop will require stronger riding during the last few strides because when he sees the drop the horse may very well hold back, and possibly drop his hind-legs. However, don't be too aggressive, and do not go too fast, just with more impulsion.

3. *Spreads*

a) Spread fences are generally easier for the horse to see and jump than uprights, especially spreads of the ascending oxer type or triple bars.

b) The most difficult spreads are true parallels.

c) Look at your spread fences on cross-country and decide into which category they fit. For example, a table is a square oxer (or true parallel) unless it is a picnic table with a built-in bench in front of it, when it becomes an ascending oxer. A log pile can be constructed as a true parallel or as an oxer. The V corner of a fence which can be jumped instead of jumping the fence as an in-and-out is sometimes constructed as a parallel and sometimes as an ascending oxer. In the latter case it is much easier to jump. (See diagram 20.) A tiger trap is really a triple bar, and so on.

d) For a triple bar or ascending oxer, ride at a normal cross-country speed, quite fast, sit down into the saddle for the last three or four strides, and drive without altering the speed of the horse too much. If you have him well in hand you can ride

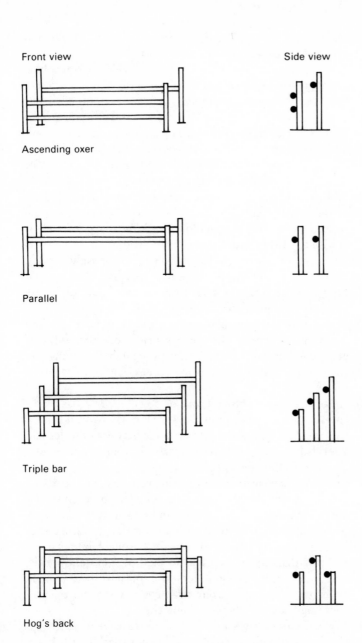

Front view   Side view

Ascending oxer

Parallel

Triple bar

Hog's back

Diagram 20 Spread fences

on into the fence without interfering, then encourage him to take off at the appropriate spot.

e) Develop your eye for a stride. This will help enormously in riding your cross-country courses. It is not that hard to do: any time when you are cantering or galloping your horse out in the fields, pick out a spot ahead — say a daisy or a little bush — decide how many strides it is till you reach that spot, and ride on to it, counting the strides. At first you will be way out, but with practice you will develop a good eye and be able to see your stride into fences from quite a long way out.

f) With spread fences, especially triple bars and big parallels, it is important to get right up to the fence and jump from the bottom pole rather than standing back. With true parallels it is wise to start preparing the horse a little farther out than is necessary for the triple bar, maybe seven or eight strides. However, do not try to check much; rather, sit down and hold him together; you want to be balanced but not to lose your cross-country speed.

g) If you have lost your good pace — maybe because of a bad jump just before the big spread, or the difficult ground — then you have to start riding forward strongly in the last few strides, and this sometimes leads to an awkward jump.

h) If the landing was difficult (maybe downhill, or it was a large spread and the horse jumped a little big) try to sit down for the next few strides and get the horse between your leg and your hand again, and so re-establish your proper cross-country rhythm and speed.

i) Once you have learned how to ride your horse forward in a good cross-country rhythm and at the right speed, and if you are riding towards a spread fence and see your stride, it is easy to ride on into it. If you do not see the stride, it is still better to try to help the horse and drive on, keeping him well up to the bit, than to check back at the last minute. Spreads, especially big ones, require lots of impulsion and are much easier to jump out of your cross-country rhythm than by checking back and show-jumping them.

j) If you are faced with a really difficult fence it is best to go absolutely straight over the middle, not checking the horse but riding him well up from your seat into your hand and maintaining your usual cross-country speed and rhythm.

4. *Ditches and water*

a) Ditches often scare the rider much more than the horse. When you walk the course take a good look at the ditches and think about the reaction your horse will have to them, and what he is likely to do.

b) Ditches, with or without fences over them, in front of them or behind them, require more impulsion and drive than fences without ditches.

c) Do not leave it too late to rebalance your horse and really put him in front of your seat and up to your hand. It is better to sit up and sit down and put your horse firmly together well back from the fence, then hold him together and increase your drive (but not necessarily your speed), in the last four or five strides.

d) Much depends on the siting of the fence. If it is straightforward, and is clearly visible from a long way off, you will probably not want to make much alteration in pace, but you must still sit up and rebalance your horse. If the fence with the ditch is hidden somewhat by the lie of the land you need to slow down as well as rebalancing your horse, because if he comes across the ditch suddenly he might spook.

e) Always approach ditches with the horse's head well up, and also your own head up, looking ahead over the fence. Nothing stops a horse quicker than the rider looking down into the ditch.

f) Between fences on cross-country, especially in a three-day event, your horse will be galloping in a long, flat, relaxed frame and you do not want to approach any fence without rebalancing him, bringing his head up, and riding his hind-end well up under him to 'coil the spring' in preparation for the fence. This is even more important in the case of ditches or water, where the rider may be hesitant and the horse might pick up this hesitancy. Above all, riders need to be determined and ride strongly forward, straight.

g) If your horse does look down at the last minute and hesitates, ride him hard forward with your seat and legs and hands and heels.

h) Make sure that you and your horse are thoroughly trained at jumping ditches. Start with very tiny ditches, no more than one foot wide and one foot deep. The depth of the ditch can make a lot of difference, and a deep ditch is much harder than a shallow one. Approach your ditch slowly, in a slow trot or even a walk. Be sure to get your horse over, no matter what it takes. I never take a young horse to a ditch the first time without a companion mounted on a trained and confident horse who can show the youngster the way. I also take along a lunge rein and lunge whip in case all else fails and I have to lunge over the ditch the first time or two. Then we go to the ditch, and we do not leave until the horse is jumping confidently over in both directions from a walk trot and canter.

i) Do not approach the ditch fast, even when you are going to canter it; keep the canter very collected and impulsive.

j) Repetition and jumping many ditches (all very small at first) of different types, sizes and depths and in all kinds of locations is the key to success. Taking the horse hunting can often help enormously in giving him (and his rider) confidence over ditches.

k) Water obstacles can range from a single shallow stream which you have to cross, with no fence, to a water splash with a fence in the middle, to a fence landing in the water and, possibly a fence out of the water. (See diagram 21.)

l) At the lower levels the water obstacle may simply mean crossing a stream, and this fence can be approached in canter, but you should check back well before the obstacle, rebalance your horse and establish a very short-striding, bouncy canter rather than galloping in.

m) Every time the footing changes — for example, from firm turf to sand or mud — this creates a problem for your horse, Remain alert to the footing, and adjust the stride accordingly.

n) If the water is deeper than six inches, or if there is a fence to be jumped in the middle or on leaving the water, TROT in, do not canter. It is a big mistake to enter water too fast.

o) If you have a fence into the water sit down and collect the horse on to a very short canter stride, or even a trot, and jump in quite slowly. The bouncing canter may be better for a less bold horse, as it is easier to maintain the impulsion. Do not jump into water fast because there is a certain concussion when the horse hits the water, and since he doesn't know how deep it is, he is liable to land stiff-legged. If the bottom is muddy the front legs may be held down, and he may not be

Walk, then trot, through large puddle or small, shallow pond.

Trot over small ditch.

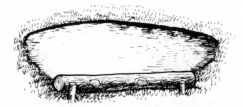

Trot through water and jump log, then trot over log into water.

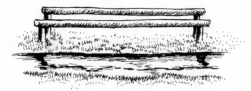

Jump ditch and log combination.

Diagram 21 *Water obstacles*

able to get his knees up to make the next stride.

p) The rider's position should be very close to the saddle so that you can drive with your seat and legs, and also absorb the shock of the landing. The upper body should not get too far forward in case the horse stumbles or pecks on landing, in which case you need to be able to get his head up and help to keep him on his feet. If all your weight comes suddenly on his shoulders, this will not help.

q) Adequate training with water long before you start competing your horse is really the key to success at water fences. Start by walking him across small streams where the water is very shallow, no more than a couple of inches deep. Include stream crossings (provided the stream is very shallow and the bottom is sand or gravel) in your daily exercise routine.

r) Next trot through the water and later canter, on a very collected stride in the water. This will allow your horse to learn that the water is no problem, the spray will not hurt him, he is not going to slip, or get his feet stuck in the mud. He will become perfectly confident in the water.

s) Next take some cavalletti to the water and practise trotting over very tiny fences in the stream and out of the stream, and finally set up a small jump into the water and make an in-and-out.

t) Even an experienced horse will benefit from a refresher course at the stream before the season begins. Keep the fences very small and only work in very shallow water; your object is to create perfect confidence in your horse, so that he doesn't even consider the water at all when he is asked to jump into it.

u) If you do not have a stream or a safe, shallow place to train in water, and cannot get to one, consider making your own. You can use any shallow depression in the ground, or dig it out slightly, line it with plastic and cover it with fine gravel, then keep it filled with a hose.

v) If you do have a fall in water your horse is likely to lose a lot of confidence, and you should return to schooling in shallow water at home.

w) Once your horse is confident about shallow water he will enjoy standing in knee-deep streams or pools, where the water flowing past his legs is very relaxing and enjoyable to him.

5. *Banks and drops*

   a) At the lower levels banks usually consist of a simple step up or down. This creates no real problem for the horse, but serves to prepare him for jumping from one level to another.

   b) When you are approaching any uphill step or bank it is vital to keep sufficient impulsion. A series of steps up, for example, requires a deal of impulsion, and speed. Sit down and take a firmer hold on the reins, and at the same time drive with your seat and legs. This will bring the hocks under your horse and enable him to push himself up the steps.

   c) Another problem with steps or banks is the balance. It is important to stay completely in balance with your horse, and especially when going up steps, not to get left behind the movement.

   d) The horse may not be able to see what is on top of a bank until he is on the top. If he suddenly sees a fence or a ditch he may put in an extra stride that you aren't expecting. This can be difficult to sit, unless you are completely in balance with your horse.

   e) Coming down off a bank, or down steps, you must still drive and hold your horse together between your legs and your hands, but you need to brace yourself to be ready for the landing and not allow your weight to come too far forward.

   f) Both going up and coming down, straightness is very important. Bring your horse in close, with sufficient impulsion and more speed than you would use for a simple upright, but otherwise treat the bank as an ordinary fence.

   g) Banks and steps and drops cause a lot of jarring to a horse, so you must be careful not to practise them too much. To jump well a horse must really enjoy it, so avoid big banks or steps or drops in training. Make sure your horse is happy popping up and down small banks, then before a competition gradually progress to one or two bigger banks, but do not over-jump them. In competition make sure you maintain your speed and increase your impulsion approaching uphill banks and you should have no problems.

   h) For the novice horse it is a good idea to trot drop fences at first: let your horse take a good look, and then just drop down gently. As your horse gains confidence, canter the approach, but keep the canter slow, on a short, bouncy stride.

   i) When you come down a drop keep a light contact on the rein, and keep your legs forward under you; your body should lean slightly forward. You need to maintain balance and contact and yet let the horse stretch his head and neck.

j) Keep the horse straight, both going up and coming down steps or drops. After landing you must rebalance and re-establish your cross-country speed.

k) In a series of steps up, the width of the steps will determine whether you must bounce up them or whether there is a stride on each one. If they are narrow enough it is probably easier to approach with more speed and bounce up. When making a stride on each step going up you need to create tremendous impulsion, because the stride naturally gets shorter each time.

6. *Combination fences*

a) At the lower levels the combination fences should be very straightforward and simple, but at the top levels of the three-day event they are often very complex and with several alternative routes.

b) When you walked the course you will have decided the exact route you plan to take through each combination fence, and you will have picked out landmarks which will put you exactly on the line you want to take.

c) When you are riding the course, especially at a three-day event, time is a considerable factor, so that everything you can do to save time helps. Any interference with the horse's galloping stride will result in slowing him down, so your goal should be to interfere as little as possible.

d) When you are approaching a combination fence you must keep a constant check that you are exactly on the line you have chosen. About a hundred yards away you should be able to line up your long-distance markers so that you know you are approaching the right spot.

e) If your horse is going at a good speed, is on the bit and balanced, you need only sit down, close the legs and hands at about four strides out from the first element to check him slightly and rebalance him, and then ride on from there.

f) The rider's position should be forward and very close to the saddle in the last few strides, but you must not get in front of the movement.

g) Between the elements of the combination you must keep the

Plate XIX. Jumping into water.
A. Horse and rider jumping into water with confidence and just the right amount of aggression. Rider is in a good position, but should look up.

Plate XIX. Jumping into water.
B. The same fence, and an equally confident horse and rider taking the slightly easier route through. The rider is sitting well and looking up.

Plate XX. The drop fence.
A. This horse and his rider jump off a bank, over a big log and down a moderate drop with great gusto and in fine form.

Plate XX. The drop fence.
B. This horse and rider are clearing a larger fence with a dry ditch and a drop on the landing side. The horse looks full of confidence and yet is listening to the rider, who is in an excellent position, not too far forward, and is already looking ahead along the track to be followed.

C. This rider has brought the horse well up to the correct take-off point for a much larger drop, full of impulsion and confidence, and both horse and rider are in a good position to make the jump efficiently and safely (see opposite).

Plate XXI. This sequence of pictures shows a very confident horse and rider going straight through the centre of a coffin combination of medium difficulty. The slope down to the ditch is not too steep, and the ditch itself is not too deep or too wide to cause any real problems.

Plate XXII. A confident and workmanlike pair on the show-jumping course.

forward drive going. Your horse should stay forward, on the bit, impulsive and balanced. He must also stay straight, and this can be a big problem with some horses.

h) The horse is straight when you can feel absolutely even pressure in both hands, and even pressure under both seat-bones. Some horses will twist the hind-quarters when jumping, and this will take them off the straight line. It is usually the result of a bad take-off, but another factor to consider is the ground. Uneven or sloping ground can make it hard to see the stride.

i) Combinations all require considerable 'riding ability', not just jumping ability on the part of the horse. At international levels combination fences will be built with difficult distances or angles or corners which often cause stops and run-outs because the rider is not riding 'with his head'.

j) Combination fences with three elements are even harder. You must be certain to maintain your line going through, and the horse moves off the line very easily, especially if the ground is uneven. You must also maintain the balance and the impulsion.

k) Combination fences which involve jumping up on to a step or bank are probably the most difficult of all, because when the horse is jumping up he always loses momentum, and the rider must therefore produce a tremendously impulsive, shortened, more bouncy stride to maintain sufficient impulsion to go on through the whole combination.

l) Preparing for combinations is best done by using a great many gymnastic jumping exercises in the training of your horse. Introduce combinations gradually, and keep them very small. Bounce jumps are taught by starting out with cavalletti set 12 ft apart and then moving on to more difficult show-jumping grids. (See section on jumping training, p. 147.)

7. *Coffin fences*

a) Coffin fences are combination fences with three elements, the middle one being a ditch. Very often they are positioned in such a way that the ditch is in the bottom of a more or less steep gulley, so that you jump the first element, go downhill to the ditch, then uphill again to the third element. (See diagram 22.)

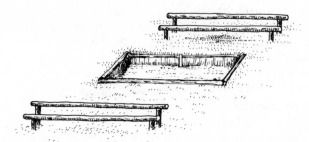

1 A coffin combination of medium difficulty placed on level ground with one stride between elements.

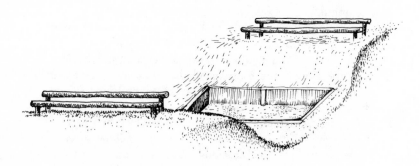

2 A coffin combination of greater difficulty because of the changing ground-levels involved.

Diagram 22. *Coffin fences*

b) Some coffins are positioned on almost level ground, and these are the easiest. The ditch is plainly visible to the horse, and there is no problem of rolling on too fast downhill into it. Nor is there the problem of the stride shortening on a steep uphill incline between the ditch and the third element.

c) The approach to the first element of the coffin is very important. If the approach is positioned just after a turn in the course, be sure to take the turn wide and use every inch of space given. It takes a very bold horse to turn in short and still have enough impulsion to jump through the coffin.

d) As with all combination fences, the line into and through the whole fence is very important. Take time to let the horse see what is ahead, collect him and approach on a shortened stride with maximum impulsion.

e) The speed you can go through will depend on the particular coffin. A flat coffin on level ground can be taken much faster than one with steep banks, but regardless of speed, you must collect and rebalance your horse, and keep him on a shorter stride with impulsion. A long stride can get you into trouble, especially with the third element.

f) With all combination fences, on cross-country or in show-jumping, look up over the first element, or first two elements, and ride for the last element. You naturally have to prepare for the first jump, but your attention and concentration should be on the final element.

g) As you ride through any combination you must not get left behind, or thrown too far forward, on landing after the first element. You need to be in a good, strong, balanced position, over the centre of gravity, with your seat close to the saddle so that you can maintain the contact and the impulsion, and if necessary drive on to the next element. If the horse is going well forward and staying on the bit you may not have to do anything, but if he starts to say no when he sees the ditch you must be in a position to drive on. The number of strides he takes is less important than that he maintains his balance and impulsion.

h) Training your horse to jump coffins should be a natural follow-on from your work with ditches. When he is jumping small ditches comfortably add a cavalletti a short distance away on the landing side, and practise the ditch followed by the cavalletti. When this is going well practise jumping a cavalletti, then a short distance — usually one stride — then the ditch. Finally, add a cavalletti on the landing side and work through the whole exercise, jump, ditch, jump.

i) Coffins are fences which create problems for the rider rather than the horse. Many riders confuse speed with impulsion, and come in on too long a stride without engaging the hindquarters of the horse. The key to success is to maintain the balance and create sufficient impulsion.

8. *Jumping into the dark*

a) On any cross-country course there are going to be places where you must jump from a possibly bright, sunny field into the woods. Sometimes the fence is very simple and straightforward, but often there is a little drop or even a stream or ditch involved.

b) The real difficulty at such fences is usually the change in light-conditions rather than the fence itself. Sit down and drive the horse more strongly into your hand than for a normal fence. Make sure you really get and keep his attention.

c) Be very sure of your line into the fence, over it and away from it. Often a jump into woods will be followed by a fairly sharp right or left turn. Provided the fence itself is straightforward, you can usually with safety angle the jump slightly, in order to put yourself on the exact line away from the fence.

d) Knowing the exact line and being on it are very important when you are in the woods. Out in the middle of a field, a few feet either side of your planned line will not make any difference, but in the woods if you are even a foot or two off your line you may run into a tree or a root or a stump.

e) Whenever you have a change of light you need to be that much more careful, more prepared, more attentive. You must prepare the horse as much as you can so that the sudden change of light does not interfere with his rhythm and concentration.

f) The most difficult fences into woods are the ones with a drop or with water. The problems here are nearly always caused by the rider coming in too fast and without enough impulsion. It is better to check back a little a few strides out, rebalance the horse, and keep him on a short, impulsive stride going well into your hand.

g) Going from darkness into light is no problem at all, because the horse can see perfectly where he is going and on almost any jump out of the woods into a nice open field he will jump well.

h) To train and prepare your horse for jumps into the darkness, and jumps set in a patch of shade beneath a tree — which is also more difficult than a fence set in an open field — practise. Canter in fields where there are plenty of dark places, hollows, or big patches of shade, and so on. This will get your horse used to listening to you and cantering on without paying too much attention to the light. Horses listen to the rider and sense from him what is ahead much more than some riders realize.

i) When you start practising jumping into the woods make sure the fences are very low and very simple at first. The novice horse needs time to gain experience and confidence before being asked any really big questions.

9. *Speed, terrain, galloping and finishing*

a) Speed will vary according to the level of the event, but in a three-day event you must go as fast as possible, consistent with being safe and jumping clean, and without taking risks.

b) When walking the course you must analyse the terrain because it is as important as the fences on cross-country. Going uphill is much more tiring for the horse than going downhill, so if the course is hilly you will want to save your horse on the uphill slopes and let him roll on downhill.

c) The weather also becomes a factor; if it is wet the going is likely to get deep and possibly slippery. You will have had a close look at the footing during your walks of the course and decided your line beforehand, but you must also be ready to change your plan later, as some stretches may have become poached and an alternative route may be less tiring.

d) Very hot, humid weather may also be a problem, as the humidity will sap the strength of your horse.

e) Before starting on cross-country, have a plan of where you are going to steady your horse and give him a breather and where you are going to push on. Then you may have to change your plan somewhat according to how your horse is feeling that day. Some days he will be full of go, and other days you may have to stir him up and create more energy.

f) If the course is relatively flat you may be able to go faster at the beginning without tiring the horse and then let him gently wind down towards the end, when he is tired. On a hilly course you must keep more horse in reserve; setting out too fast can mean that you run out of horse half-way round.

g) Ride the whole of the speed and endurance phase with the last fence of cross-country in mind. If you do not arrive at, and safely negotiate, the last fence of phase D and cross the finish-line, everything has been wasted.

h) Do not come off the cross-country course beating your horse on to make up lost seconds. By that stage it is really too late, and your horse is tired. If you have prepared correctly, made your calculations of exactly how much time you have for each kilometre of the course, and ridden sensibly, checking your watch at the appropriate points, you should be able to come over the last fence and coast home. Most often you see this bad riding at one-day events, where it is quite unnecessary and just a form of showing off.

i) Remember, if you are riding your first three-day event, that you must ride up and ask permission to dismount from the steward at the scales and then weigh in. Many first-time three-day eventers have been eliminated for forgetting to ask permission to dismount in the relief and excitement of having finished the course.

Preparing and riding phase A — roads and tracks

1. If you are riding in a three-day event the speed and endurance phase will start with phase A, roads and tracks. This is your warm-up for the steeplechase, phase B.

2. When you are driving the roads and tracks at the official course walk pay particular attention to the terrain. You will want to give your horse a pipe-opener on phase A to prepare him for the steeplechase. Phase A is about four kilometres, and, depending on the terrain, you want this 200-metre pipe-opener about two and a half kilometres before the end of phase A.

3. Your time allows you about four minutes for each kilometre, but phase A runs straight into phase B, the steeplechase, so it is up to you to gain the extra time you need in case there are any adjustments you must make to your tack or your horse before starting on the steeplechase. Usually you will want about two minutes at the end of phase A before you start on phase B, so plan to finish A two minutes early.

4. You cannot be too organized for a three-day event. You should have a definite plan, either written down or in your head, of exactly how fast you are going to ride each kilometre, where you will save your horse, and where you will push on. You need a good stopwatch that is easy to operate and easy to read. Some people use the specially designed eventing watches which combine an ordinary watch with a stopwatch; others use an ordinary watch on one wrist and a stopwatch on the other. Since you have four phases to ride against the clock, it is essential to devise a system of timekeeping which will work, and which you can check easily as you ride along.

5. Be at the start of phase A about ten minutes ahead of your time to start. This gives you time to organize yourself, weigh-out — if it applies to you — check your horse one last time and get mounted. You do not need to mount until a couple of minutes before you start.

6. If you are riding a horse that is protected by bandages they should be sewn and taped in place. Whether you put bandages on or not will probably depend on the course. If there is water early on in the course bandages will become waterlogged at that point, and may be best avoided. Most people use some form of leg-protection, at least on the front legs. If bandages are not appropriate because of the water, or deep mud, over-reach boots (bell boots) and brushing boots (shin boots) are good protection for the front legs.

7. Studs are a tremendous help also, for both steeplechase and cross-country, and are usually no hindrance on roads and tracks, unless you are obliged to ride on a metalled road (which is fortunately rare).

8. Before mounting for the start of phase A take a final check round your horse, including studs, boots, bandages, girth and surcingle (overgirth), then mount and be ready to set out on the first phase.

9. To make up the time you want between phases A and B you may want to set off on phase A rather faster, and do the final two kilometres rather slower. A trot is the usual gait for roads and tracks, but some horses are not happy being held back to trot at this stage, and are more relaxed if allowed to canter along gently. Do not waste your horse's energy, or your own, fighting to stay in trot if the horse is happier cantering.

10. After one or two kilometres warm-up and a couple of hundred

metres half-speed gallop as a pipe-opener you should be able to complete phase A in a relaxed trot, and still have two minutes in hand before the start of phase B. During the time you are getting yourself and your horse ready and fit to compete in your first three-day event you must learn about your horse thoroughly, then ride the horse as he is. If he is highly excitable and liable to fight and leap around and waste energy waiting to go into the starting-box for phase B you will not want to have so much time in hand — thirty seconds will probably be ample in that case.

11. During the last kilometre of phase A you can walk and shorten your stirrups a hole or two in preparation for the steeplechase. When you finish phase A do not forget to punch your watch and keep your horse moving gently in walk. Make any adjustments to your tack, mentally ride the steeplechase, reviewing where the quarter, half and three-quarter markers are, and how much time you have for each kilometre. The steeplechase is about four kilometres.

12. Have someone to meet you at the end of phase A with spare equipment (stirrup leathers, reins, etc.) in case you have any problems, and also to tell you how the steeplechase is riding. Your knowledgeable helper can sponge your horse's mouth, check the bandages and studs, and if necessary help you into the starting-box.

Preparing and riding phase B — steeplechase

1. The steeplechase phase of a three-day event is different from a normal steeplechase in that it is NOT a race. Each horse competes individually, against the clock. The speed will vary according to the level from 640 to 690 metres per minute.

2. The fences for steeplechase in a three-day event should be standard, with the fixed and solid part of all obstacles not to exceed one metre (3′ 3″) in height, and the brush not to exceed an overall height of 1·30 metres (4′ 3″). The spread will vary according to the level of competition from 1·40 m (4′ 7″) to 5′ 11″ at the highest point, and 6′ 7″ to 9′ 2″ at the base. The brush may be anything from soft evergreen material to stiff, solid-looking birch.

3. The steeplechase phase tests the horse's ability to jump clean and fast, expending as little energy as possible. Every fence will be approximately the same, and there should be no tricks or twisty turns.

4. Timing and precise riding are very important. You did not put in all the hard work and months of preparation for this three-day event to have unnecessary time faults on the steeplechase phase; however, you do not want to come in ahead of the time, as this will tire your horse without reason.

5. It is very important to keep track of exactly where you are on the course and of the seconds already elapsed, and to check that you are keeping to your plan.

6. The rider's position should be very balanced, behind and not over the withers, which will allow the horse the freedom to jump up and out in front, and as still and close to the horse as possible.

7. You must ride your horse straight, forward and fast, but always in balance and on contact.

8. You can and should train your horse for the steeplechase phase. Too many people seem to ignore this and hope it will go all right on the day. It is not necessary to construct a whole steeplechase course to practise over, but either construct a couple of regulation fences or take your horse to a farm where you can practise over a couple of fences. Event horses jump so many unusual fences that the straightforward racing fences often seem to raise their suspicions, and many will back off a bit and jump the first fence too slowly and carefully unless they are ridden on strongly.

9. Training over the steeplechase fences, either on your own or beside another horse, can help a lot in teaching your horse about jumping economically at speed.

10. When walking the steeplechase pay particular attention to the half-way marker — you must know exactly where it is. Most steeplechase courses are twice around, so the half-way marker is actually the quarter-way marker, and when you pass the starting-box you are half-way through your ride.

11. You may want to pace off the distance from the mid-way point between the last two fences and the finish. When you know how many metres this is you can compute how many seconds you have in hand at that point, and use it as a final check during the competition.

12. In planning your time on steeplechase it is an enormous help if you know your horse well. Some horses are slow out of the box and pick up speed steadily all the way round, while others may not settle until they are a little tired, and others may gallop the whole course right out of stride.

13. In order not to interfere with your start it is a good idea to punch your watch five seconds before the 'off'. Check your time at the quarter-marker, remembering your watch is five seconds ahead of your real time, and try to be exactly on time at that point. Half-way around the course — which is probably at the finish of one circuit — you should be ten seconds ahead of your scheduled time. Most horses will travel slightly slower during the second circuit, and you do not want to have to drive your horse unnecessarily.

14. By the three-quarter marker you will probably be only three seconds ahead of your scheduled time. If you have measured off the distance from between the last two fences to the finish-line you can check your watch again at that point to know whether you are keeping a steady pace or must ride slightly harder for the finish.

15. Try to finish as close to the optimum time as possible. One second early is going to avoid penalty points just as well as thirty seconds, and finishing with so much time in hand just cooks your horse without reason.

16. The rider's job on steeplechase, as in all the phases of the three-day event, is to give the horse the steadiest, most accurate ride possible. The quieter you are on his back, the easier it will be for him.

17. During phases A, B and C you must keep remembering that the most demanding part of the day, phase D, the cross-country, is still to come, so try to save your horse as much as possible.

18. Adjustments that may have to be made as you ride the steeplechase course should be made as quietly and easily as possible. The greater the speed of the horse the more delicate his balance, so stay as still and quiet as you can, consistent with keeping as close to your time as possible.

19. If you do not make the time on steeplechase do not worry about it. Sometimes, even if you ride according to your plan, the horse simply cannot make the speed. Perhaps the footing was bad for him, or the turns too sharp. Do not waste time or energy worrying about it afterwards. That phase is over now, and your next concern is to get your horse through phase C and back to the vet-box at the start of cross-country with the least stress possible.

20. Remember that to go well round the steeplechase course the horse must be very strongly in your hand so that he draws into

the fences, right from the start. If he is not strongly in your hand you must take appropriate action to put him there with your driving aids.

21. The end of the steeplechase is also the start of phase C, the second roads and tracks. Remember to punch your watch, check your time on steeplechase, and restart the watch for phase C.

22. Do not pull your horse up suddenly as you come off the steeplechase but allow him to wind down gradually, from a gallop to a canter to a trot. This is better for his legs, and also gets you a good start on phase C.

23. Most organizers provide a holding area some distance beyond the finish of steeplechase where you can get off your horse if you wish, check his shoes and rinse out his mouth with a sponge and douse cold water under his tail. If your horse is young he will probably come off the steeplechase very leg-weary and you should then take advantage of this opportunity to freshen him up. Hopefully the holding area will be at least five hundred metres from the end of phase B to allow your horse to wind down gradually.

24. Have your groom waiting at the appropriate point with a bucket of water and a sponge, and an easy-boot, in case your horse has lost a shoe. It should not take more than 90 seconds to check his feet, wash out his mouth and, if it is very hot, rinse under his tail with cool water. You do not have to dismount, and probably should stay on board. You can loosen the girth and over-girth, and start walking on even while your groom is still working on your horse.

Riding phase C — roads and tracks

1. Normally you will want to walk the first five minutes of phase C and make up the time later, especially if you are riding a young or inexperienced horse. The speed on phase C is the same as phase A — i.e., 220 metres per minute. At a good trot your horse will easily cover a kilometre in four minutes, and if you have prepared your plan correctly you will have allowed seven minutes or so for the first kilometre to permit you to walk.

2. Pay attention to the footing on phase C; if it is bad, walk in those places. You can make the time up elsewhere when the footing improves. You want to finish phase C without time penalties, but you do not want to risk losing a shoe or laming your horse on the way.

3. When you really know your horse and have a lot of experience yourself you may find that some horses do better if you come off steeplechase and continue to canter for five hundred metres or so, if the ground is flat and the footing good. This gives you a good start on phase C. After cantering some distance let your horse settle into a good trot and get his rhythm. After five or six kilometres bring him down to a walk and make sure that he gets a good breather.

4. Every horse is different, and you must learn what works best for your particular horse. If he comes off steeplechase exhausted, then you *must* walk until he recovers, but if he feels pretty strong he may actually do better if you do not break his rhythm at that point.

5. Knowing your own horse, and benefiting from your past experience, you should have decided beforehand on your plan of action for both normal circumstances and for the unforeseen. Ride phase C according to your plan, and keep yourself alert and focused on the job in hand. This energetic alertness of yours will influence your horse and keep him up to the bit and waiting for the next challenge.

6. The only disadvantage to the brief check at the end of steeplechase is that it breaks the horse's rhythm and sometimes makes him think his job is over. The walking at the start of phase C tends to confirm this idea in his mind, and it may be difficult to stir him up again and produce the necessary energy and enthusiasm to accomplish phase D.

7. The end of phase C is the vet-box or 'pocket' where you spend the compulsory ten-minute break and the official vets will check your horse to ensure his fitness to continue on phase D. It is worth planning phase C so that you finish two minutes early, and can actually spend twelve minutes in the box instead of ten. The extra two minutes is more valuable to you here than on phase C.

8. As you come within range of the vet-box try to catch the eye of one of the vets who is not busy so that he can watch you jog your horse in off phase C. Most horses jog better when mounted, and this also saves time in the vet-box.

9. Remember to punch your watch and check your time as you cross the finish-line of phase C.

What to do in the vet-box

1. As soon as you cross the finish-line of phase C you are free to

dismount, loosen the girth and take off your horse's brushing boots while the vet is checking his temperature, pulse and respiration.

2. When you first come into the vet-box make yourself known to the starter, or other officials keeping times on the horses in the box. Ask how much time you have, and set your watch to keep track of it yourself.

3. You need several people waiting at the vet-box to help you. Four or five can work on your horse at the same time. You do not have to take off the tack, but you do have time to do so, and it usually helps if you take off at least the saddle. Your grooms will need two or three buckets of water, sponges, sweat-scrapers and towels as well as spare tack, studs and an easy-boot for emergency use.

4. The important thing is to cool the horse down. If you have several people, two can work on each side. The horse can be thoroughly doused with water on his neck, chest, back, tummy and hind-quarters by one person, while another follows with a sweat-scraper and a towel. If it is hot, sponge with cool water under his tail, and also on his head. Removing the bridle saves getting your tack all wet, and washing your horse's head and face can cool him off fast.

5. After this quick wash-down a sweat-sheet should be put on the horse, or, if it is cold, a wool cooler, and as soon as his legs have been washed and dried and his feet checked he should be kept walking. If he is wearing bandages take care to keep them dry.

6. If the horse has lost any studs, or the studs are to be changed, it should be done right away and he should then be walked slowly.

7. Another reason for having several people work on your horse at one time is that the job can be done much more quickly, and he will not be kept standing still for more than a minute or so. He should be kept walking quietly, so far as possible, and if he must be stood still, head him into the wind (unless it is bitter cold), as this will help him get his breath back.

8. You must keep track of your time but you will perhaps have a coach or some friends in the box who will tell you how the course is riding.

9. When you have three minutes left have your grooms finish tacking up the horse and find the vet to give you a final go-ahead on him.

10. If all your training has been properly carried out you should have

no problem so far as fitness is concerned. However, problems can arise on the steeplechase, or the weather may be extreme and have affected your horse adversely. If the vet advises you NOT to take your horse on cross-country you should accept that decision. It is terribly disappointing to have to withdraw in the box, but it is better to save your horse to run another day than to go ahead against professional advice and break him down for good.

11. If all goes well you should get on your horse one minute before your starting-time on phase D and proceed to the starting-box. Many people smear the horse's legs, chest and belly with a thick coating of Vaseline at this point in the hope that if he hits a fence it will help to make him slide off, and also will act as some protection against splinters, thorns, mud and water.

12. Go quietly into the starting-box about fifteen seconds before the off, and despite the excitement and tension mounting inside you, try to remain calm, and totally concentrated on the job at hand. Your calm attitude will help to keep your horse relaxed and concentrated, and so avoid all possibility of a false start.

13. As at the commencement of steeplechase, if you punch your stopwatch five seconds before the 'off' it will not interfere with your start and you will be able to concentrate more fully on getting away from the starting-box and making a good, strong approach to the first fence.

14. If you should be unlucky enough to have a stop or a fall on cross-country you will have to decide whether to try to make up the time by running your horse flat out afterwards. Since the fall will almost certainly have shaken his confidence (not to mention yours), it may be best to take your time and not try to rush on right away. Once he has regained his confidence in his jumping ability he will let you know he is ready to go on full strength again.

15. Remember that corners, hills up and down, and rough or uneven footing are just as difficult for the horse to cope with as are the fences. The basic essential for good cornering is to have the horse very well balanced and hold him between your leg and your hand. If you need to check, do so before the corner, and then accelerate round it. If you pull your horse round a corner unbalanced you will lose control afterwards.

16. When you are going downhill the thing to remember is that the horse is much better at it than the rider. It seldom bothers a

horse to go rolling on down a hill, but it may give you a problem at the bottom if there is a fence or a sharp turn. However, concentrate on getting down the hill first — preferably straight down, as this puts less strain on the legs — then check, and make the turn or approach the fence.

17. Going uphill, try to save your horse. Keep him well balanced between the leg and the hand, and if there is a fence at the top approach it with as much impulsion as possible. Don't let your horse sprawl, and he will jump much better than you thought possible.

Care of your horse after cross-country

1. At whatever level you are riding, when you come off cross-country the welfare of your horse is your first consideration.
2. If your competition is a one-day event the cross-country is usually the final phase. Make your way without delay to your trailer or temporary stabling and remove the tack and bandages and wash the horse down carefully and thoroughly.
3. Look for any little injuries, cuts or thorns, and attend to them at once.
4. When you have washed your horse use the sweat-scraper and sponge to dry him as much as possible, put on a sweat-sheet or wool cooler, and walk him dry.
5. Put his bandages on with a cooling lotion and plenty of gamgee or cotton; place his travelling rug over the string-mesh sweat-sheet; remove his studs, and pack the holes with cotton soaked with oil; then give him a short drink.
6. If possible this first drink should contain a double handful of glucose powder in order to restore his energy and keep him happy.
7. Load him into your horse-box or trailer, with a full net of hay (unless you are staying overnight at the event location) and take him home as soon as possible.
8. Make sure your horse knows that you are pleased with his performance. Praise him a lot, and stroke him. He will appreciate your happiness with him and will remember it.
9. The sooner you can take him home the better. Standing around in the trailer for an hour or so only gives him a chance to chill and stiffen up.
10. Have a boiled feed waiting for him at home. You can boil barley

and a handful of linseed, or just boil his oats. Add this to some bran to make a delicious bran mash.

11. After he has eaten check him once more. Remove the sweat-sheet and brush him lightly over and replace his night rug. Then leave him in peace with a full net of hay and plenty of fresh, clean water for a good night's rest.

12. The next day walk him out quietly to get rid of any stiffness. Have him trotted up so that you can make sure he is sound, and feel for any heat in his feet and legs. If all is well he can resume his training routine the next day, but it should be kept short and with little stress. The third day he should be back in full training.

13. If your competition was a three-day event your procedure will be a little different. Take your horse back to the stables promptly and wash him down. Inspect him carefully for cuts and bruises. You will know if you hit a fence hard, and where he is likely to have been hurt.

14. Make sure you check your horse very thoroughly and deal with any injuries.

15. Apply a cooling lotion and bandages to his legs and walk him dry in a sweat-sheet, wool cooler, or sweat-sheet under his regular rug, depending on the weather.

16. He can have a short drink immediately after you have washed him, and again put some glucose into it. Give him some hay, and leave him to rest for an hour.

17. Feed him, and after he has eaten take off his bandages and rugs and take him outside to check that he is still sound. Feel his legs and feet very carefully for any signs of heat, pain or swelling.

18. If your horse shows any signs of lameness and you cannot find the reason for it, call the veterinary surgeon. It is his job to help all the competitors to have their horses sound enough to pass the veterinary inspection the next morning.

19. If your horse is sound and there is no heat or swelling anywhere, put him back in his box stall, reapply the cooling lotion (or some people like to use Animalintex or other poultice) to his legs and rebandage. Make sure he is appropriately rugged up, and leave him with his hay and water until you check him again last thing that night.

20. If he has a problem you may have to work on him all night to get him ready for the examination next morning. Cold-water hosing can be tremendously effective, especially when combined with gentle slow walking, in preventing swelling and stiffness.

Remember, if your horse stands still all night with an injured leg he is bound to be swollen and stiff by morning, and he will not pass the veterinary check before the show-jumping.

21. The vets will pass horses one would normally not consider sound, but who can obviously jump the course without suffering from it. They will only 'spin', or eliminate, horses that are badly lame and obviously incapable of jumping.

22. If your horse has not suffered any injury, allow him to rest well during the night but get him out early next morning to check him again. Usually ten minutes' cold hosing and half an hour's gentle walking will take care of any filling in his legs and stiffness in his body.

23. The veterinary check is usually at 9.30 or 10.0 a.m., which gives you plenty of time for hosing, walking, feeding, a gentle grooming and if necessary more walking before you have to present your horse to the panel. When you do run him up in front of the panel be sure to keep him on a tight rein.

24. After passing the veterinary inspection you can return your horse to his box stall, where your groom can tidy him up and plait his mane ready for the parade of competitors and the final phase of the three-day event, the show-jumping. While this is being done you should inspect the show-jumping course, learn it thoroughly, assess all its problems and decide how you will ride it, always bearing in mind that your horse may be a little tired and lack some of his usual athletic ability.

PART FOUR
Show-jumping

Purpose

1. In a three-day event the purpose of the show-jumping is to prove that, on the day after a severe test of endurance, the horses are actually capable of show-jumping. They must be supple, energetic, athletic and obedient.
2. The riders must prove their ability to be accurate over show-jumping fences, which are easily knocked down and which, although not enormous (the maximum height is 1·80 m, or 3′ 11″), are built to be massive and imposing.
3. In horse trials and one-day events, the purpose of the show-jumping phase is to prove that horse and rider can jump a course in a controlled, supple, athletic and obedient manner in a confined space. Show-jumping requires more accuracy and more refinement of control from both horse and rider than cross-country jumping.

Basic problems

1. The nature of the course, length, speed, size of fences, will depend on the level of the whole competition.
2. At the lower levels the course will be straightforward and flowing, and at the higher levels much more will be demanded of horse and rider.
3. In a three-day event the show-jumping track will be more winding, with changes of direction and doubles and trebles. There will probably also be a water jump.

Early training

1. Jumping over very small obstacles is a valuable part of the early training of every young horse.

2. Loose-jumping will improve natural balance, teach your horse to be athletic, and give him confidence.
3. Most horses really enjoy jumping loose, and it helps to prevent boredom and develop muscles.
4. Loose-jumping may be done in an indoor arena, a small outdoor arena or paddock, or, best of all, in an oval jumping lane.
5. Before starting the loose-jumping, get your horse accustomed to following you as you lead him over small obstacles, both in the school and out in the fields. A pole in a gateway, a small ditch or log in the field, will help to prepare him for what is ahead.
6. Teach your horse to trot over trotting poles. Start with a single pole on the ground and walk over it several times in both directions. Then add two more poles, so that you have a line of three poles placed 4' 6" apart. Walk through from both directions and then trot through, repeating the exercise until the horse moves freely and willingly forward and over the poles in a good, rhythmic trot, slightly increasing his impulsion as he goes through.
7. Ride through trotting poles at rising trot at first. The action of rising will help to accentuate the rhythm for the horse, and will also ensure that you are well forward and out of the saddle sufficiently so that you do not bump the horse's back.
8. Trotting poles will also help in muscling up your horse and preparing him for the more strenuous work of jumping.

The jumping lane

1. The best way to loose-jump is in an oval jumping lane. There are also straight jumping lanes, but oval lanes have the advantage of discouraging the horse from rushing.
2. With an oval lane the trainer can simply walk round in the centre, keeping the horse going around the lane, with a lunge whip.
3. The jumping lane should not be too big or the trainer will have trouble keeping the horse going. Nor should it be too small, or there will be no possibility of the horse getting a straight approach to any fence. An ideal size would be about 25m to 30m long by 15m to 20m wide.
4. The track where the jumps will be set should be 3m to 4m wide.
5. There should be a continuous fence, preferably 2m to 2.50m round the outside of the oval. There may be a continuous fence, or a partial fence, or sheep hurdles, around the inside of the track. In any case, the inside fence need not be so high as the outside.

6. Horses usually enjoy the jumping lane very much once they get the idea, and the trainer usually has no difficulty keeping the horse going around.

The fences and the footing

1. The fences (jumps) in the lane should be solid and as varied as possible, and the heights and widths should be easily adjustable.
2. Solid fences encourage good, clean jumping from the start. Flimsy fences encourage careless jumping, and horses are well aware of the solidity of the jumps.
3. Include at least one ditch in the lane. This should be narrow and shallow, but properly built, with reinforced sides.
4. There should be the possibility of erecting parallel rails, for width, and an in-and-out, for use later on in the training.
5. One method of holding the poles in place is to sink two upright posts on each side of the track, about six inches apart, at the places where you want to erect fences. Bore holes through both posts at six-inch intervals and put iron pins through both posts. The jumping poles will rest on the iron pins, between the two posts. To increase the height, raise the pole and the pin to the hole above or add more pins and poles.
6. Footing is of great importance any time you are jumping a horse. The footing in the lane should be a properly prepared surface which is resilient, not too firm, not deep, and never slippery.
7. Start out by sending your horse around the lane with no fences in it at all. Allow the horse to go around several times in each direction. To change direction, stop the horse, take him out of the lane and reverse him and then start again. The horse could easily turn around in the lane, but it is not a good idea to let him do this in case he got the idea of reversing himself without being asked to do so by his trainer.
8. When the horse is used to the lane without jumps in it, and goes round confidently in trot and in canter, introduce one or two low jumps. Cross-rails are a very good idea at the start. If you use verticals, keep them to about one foot in height with a good ground line.
9. Gradually raise the fences over a period of a week or two until they are about two feet six inches, and introduce at least one spread — preferably an ascending oxer — starting at about two feet wide and gradually increasing it to four feet wide.

10. Send the horse round two or three times until he is going calmly and jumping well, in stride, then stop him and quietly reward him. Then reverse and send him round the other way. The horse's balance will improve very rapidly, and he will become more eager in his mounted work as a result.

11. If you do not have access to a jumping lane a similar result can be achieved in an indoor arena (if it is fairly small, just put one or two fences on one long side at first) or in an outdoor arena or small paddock.

Lungeing over fences

1. If you cannot construct anything for loose-jumping, lungeing over fences can be a very useful substitute.

2. It may be continued throughout the life of the horse. Not only is it a good way to teach a horse to jump, but it is also a good way to correct faults or carry training further.

3. It allows the trainer to watch the horse throughout every phase of the jump, and also to jump him without the added weight of a rider.

4. It is a valuable means of restoring confidence in a horse who has lost it.

5. It will improve balance and impulsion and teach the horse to jump smoothly, in-stride and without rushing.

6. Lungeing is usually done from the cavesson or halter, and the horse may or may not be wearing a saddle and bridle. You should NEVER lunge over fences with side reins or a chambon, or any other gadget on the horse.

7. Whenever you jump a horse it is advisable to fit on him boots or bandages, at least to the front legs, for protection and to avoid bumps and bruises, and the possibility of starting up a splint.

8. Place one side of the fence you are lungeing over up close to a wall or fence-line. At the other side of the jump, the side nearest the trainer, there should be a wing consisting of a long pole with one end on the ground and the other end on the top of the standard supporting the jump. The lunge-line will slide freely up this pole as the horse jumps, and cannot become caught or entangled on any part of the jump.

9. When lungeing over fences be sure to keep your hand very steady and quiet on the line. Do not suddenly throw the lunge-line up into the air as the horse jumps, since this sudden movement will

cause him to raise his head and neck over the fence instead of lowering and stretching it.

10. Start lungeing with no jump at all between the standards. Lunge the horse on a circle near the standards, but not passing between them at first. When the horse is going freely in trot with a good rhythm and without rushing, gradually move forward, towards the jump, and allow him to make a slightly larger circle which will bring him beyond the wing and between the standards.

11. Keep very calm and quiet when lungeing. Do not wave or crack the whip or frighten the horse in any way. If the horse is reluctant to go between the standards drop behind him to a stronger driving position and use your voice and the whip to encourage him quietly.

12. When the horse is going calmly and rhythmically between the standards add a pole on the ground. Gradually build your jump until it is about a foot high. Remember to change your wing pole each time you change direction, and to work equally on the right and left rein.

13. Gradually raise the fence, up to about 2′ 6″, and add to it and vary it. Make it into a spread, since spreads are particularly valuable in the development of the correct muscles, and in teaching the horse to jump off his hocks.

14. If you have never lunged over fences, start out by practising with an experienced horse, and make sure you can do it well before trying to lunge a young, green horse over fences.

15. Take care to ensure that the horse has complete freedom of his head and neck over the fence. Do not jerk him back suddenly on landing. It is natural for the horse to land moving faster forward; probably he will land in canter even if the approach was in trot. You must bring him back to trot gently and quietly, avoiding any sudden jerks or stops, as these are not only bad for his training but potentially very dangerous for his legs.

16. Lungeing over fences should mostly be done in trot. Trotting small jumps develops correct use of the hind-quarters and more accuracy than jumping at canter. It also prevents the horse getting over-excited and learning to rush his fences. Later in the horse's training, lungeing over fences in canter can also be used, but at this early stage of training the trot is more valuable. If the horse breaks into a canter one stride before the jump, however, you should not try to interfere. It is too late to make any further adjustments, and you will distract him and put him off balance.

Long-reining over fences

1. Long-reining, or lungeing with two reins (the inside rein direct to the trainer's hand, the outside rein passing around the far side of the horse and behind him, above the hocks) may also be practised over fences.
2. Long-reining is especially useful for a horse who gets over-excited when jumping on the lunge, since it allows the trainer more control of pace and rhythm.
3. Do no attempt to long-rein over fences until you are thoroughly proficient on the flat.
4. Never pass the inside rein through the stirrup when long-reining over fences: it should always come direct to the trainer's hand. This allows more freedom of the horse's head and neck during the jump.

Basic objectives

1. In loose-jumping, lungeing or long-reining over fences the basic objectives are the same — i.e.:
   a) The horse should gain confidence.
   b) The horse should learn obedience.
   c) The horse should increase his athletic ability through gymnastic exercises.
2. Do not try to do too much too quickly. Make sure the lessons are short, enjoyable and encouraging for the young horse.

Jumping when mounted

1. Do not overlook the importance of trotting poles, discussed in the section Early Training 6, 7 and 8, p. 148. For the horse, carrying a rider over fences involves adapting and rebalancing himself in order to adjust to carrying the weight of the rider. It should not be a cause of fear or over-excitement.
2. For the horse to jump involves several clear stages. First he will lower his head and neck on the approach, then he will shorten his neck and raise his head, and, with his hocks well under him, he will lever his forehand off the ground. The next stage of the jump involves stretching out his head and neck as he springs upward and forward. In suspension, his head and neck will be stretched fully forward and down. His hind-legs are then gathered up under his belly. In landing, he brings his head and neck up, and stretches his forefeet down to the ground.

3. Once you can trot your horse through three trotting poles in good rhythm, relaxed, and going straight through the centre of the line of poles, you can add a small cross-rail beyond the poles. The distance between the trotting poles for most horses will be 4½ feet. Double this distance and set your cross-rail very low, nine feet from the last pole.

4. It is important to work equally in both directions, so you may find it easiest to set the exercise in the centre of your arena. Trot through the poles, rising to the trot, keep your legs on the horse and your seat out of the saddle while the horse jumps the cross-rail, and continue in a straight line after the fence. If the horse lands in canter bring him back to trot before the end of the arena, and turn to the right the first time and to the left the next, and so on.

5. The horse should gradually increase his impulsion through the trotting poles. He should use a more active, elevated stride and his head and neck should be quite low so that he can look at the poles. The rider should maintain a quiet, soft contact with the horse's mouth without in any way interfering with his forward movement.

6. Rising to the trot at this stage helps the rider to avoid interfering in any way with the horse's natural movement and enjoyment with either his weight or his hands. A rider on a green horse should hook one finger through the martingale strap, or use a neck strap to catch hold of, or at least hold on to the mane when jumping small fences at first. The horse should enjoy jumping, and it is important to foster this enjoyment.

7. After a week or so of working through the trotting poles and small cross-rail you should have established a good rhythm and lots of confidence. Now you can increase the size of the little jump by adding a vertical rail behind the cross-rail, making a tiny spread, about 2 feet or less spread, and 18 inches in height.

8. Work through the exercise some more, in both directions, and gradually raise the little fence until it is 2 feet 6 inches high with a spread of 3 feet.

9. At the same time that you are working these exercises in your schooling sessions you can be riding your horse over poles, small logs, and small ditches outside. After two or three weeks try larger tree-trunks, slightly wider ditches, but do not get excited about jumping and do not rush your horse about when you are practising.

Gymnastic exercises

1. Most of your jumping should be done from a trot at this stage. Trot is less effort for the horse than jumping from a walk, and less exciting than jumping from the canter. It is also better in the early stages to increase the size of the jumps by widening them rather than by making them higher. In order to jump the necessary width the horse will jump higher anyway. Jumping from the trot will also teach him to use his hocks properly, and it is easier for him to judge his take-off.

2. Gymnastic jumping covers the whole field of training, from the trotting poles and small fence to very complex exercises suitable for more experienced jumpers.

3. The size of the fences is very important. During the first year of jumping the jumps should be kept very small but varied as much as possible. A young hunter or eventer should not go beyond 3' 6" in height and 8' in width during his first year. A pony should not be asked to jump more than about 2' 6" in height, and perhaps 4' in width.

4. Jumping should be fun for the horse, and never associated with pain of any sort. Approach all fences with the horse straight and well between your leg and your hand. The corner before the fence is very important. How well you ride it determines the value of your approach. Place your fences so that you have plenty of room to make a good approach. Tricky approaches and irregular distances have no place in the early schooling.

5. The landing side of a fence is just as important as the take-off. The horse should move away from the fence straight and quiet. No rushing off, no bucking, no sudden turns to right or left.

6. Small grids are very good gymnastic exercises for young horses. Keep the fences small and the distances easy. You can build up on your three trotting poles and single small spread set nine feet beyond the third pole by adding another small vertical at 18 to 20 feet (depending on the size of your horse, this should be one comfortable stride after the trot fence). Then add another fence, say thirty feet beyond, to give two cantering strides in between.

7. Gymnastic jumping is much misunderstood. It really covers any jumping exercises where the horse is made to use himself to the fullest. For example, the gymnastic exercise might start off with trotting poles and a small trot fence and continue with two cantering fences, all on a straight line, at the end of which the horse might be asked to halt four seconds. Then continue in

canter, make a left turn and jump a 24 ft in-and-out in canter, after which he might be asked to trot, make a right turn and trot over a vertical and come to a walk, and so on. In other words, the whole exercise requires him to remain calm, obedient, supple and impulsive and completely under the control of his rider.

Fence construction and variety

1. Schooling fences should be solid and well built. They should have a wide 'face', and if they are not placed against a fence-line or wall but are 'island' fences they should have wings at first.
2. Although the height and width of the fences should be kept small, the more variety you can introduce the better. Jump small banks or steps, up and down, small walls, coloured poles, wet ditches, dry ditches, blind ditches, cavalletti, easy fences, up-and-down slopes, small, easy in-and-out fences.
3. It is impossible to over-emphasize the importance of jumping ditches. If possible have an older horse along with you to give your young horse confidence. At first the young horse can be allowed to follow the older one, and when he has the confidence he should be asked to jump on his own. Sometimes he should be asked to jump beside his friend, sometimes in front of him, sometimes following, so that he will develop calmness and confidence and obedience all together.
4. Jumping plenty of spread fences from a trot will ensure that the horse is active and developing the necessary muscles, and also learning to place himself correctly at his fences.
5. Over-facing a young horse at this stage will result in teaching him to refuse instead of developing the habit of jumping whatever he is asked. Jumping is simply moving forward in the direction his rider is asking him to go, regardless of the fact that there is a small obstacle in the way.
6. Do not be in a hurry to start jumping from the canter. If you are jumping small grids the horse will learn about taking off from the canter in the middle sections of the grid, but it is wise to keep the first fence at a trot for some time.
7. It is always easy enough to make a horse jump faster, but it is often difficult to slow down a 'rusher'.
8. If you are using a jumping grid and find that it is too exciting for your horse (which may be the case with a Thoroughbred) go back to individual small fences in the trot, and when you are ready to start jumping in the canter place one small cross-rail on the

perimeter of a large circle and canter round the circle, sometimes jumping, sometimes passing the fence.

9. If your horse is the sluggish type and needs to be made to move more freely forward, jumping 'grids' will help to improve his activity, balance and rhythm.

10. Jumping small fences outside in canter, ride the horse sufficiently strongly to make him take off well back from his fences, but do not hurry him. You want him to jump in good style, with a calm and cadenced stride both before and after the jump. Keep the horse straight and balanced and moving straight forward between your legs and your hands. Stay lightly in contact with his mouth during the approach but keep your hands low and forward and very giving so that his head is virtually free over the top of the jump, and yet you can take up a soft contact again immediately upon landing.

11. Do everything possible to make certain that your horse enjoys his jumping but does not get over-excited by it.

12. Many people like to take young event horses out with hounds, and by this stage of his training he may certainly be asked to go out for an hour or two. Preferably take along a steady companion and 'hilltop' rather than 'hunt'. Do not overstrain or overtire a young horse.

13. By this stage of his training the young horse might also go to one or two beginner shows or hunter trials, providing he is jumping well and in good style. Do not enter any class where the jumps will exceed three feet.

14. These outings help to keep your horse fresh, alert and interested in life and avoid boredom or sourness with his work at home in the ring.

Training timetable

1. The jumping and the dressage training should continue side by side. Good jumping is largely achieved on the flat and not over jumps at all, but introducing jumping into the weekly schedule helps keep the horse fresh and attentive, and at the same time introduces him to a great variety of obstacles.

2. Your training programme is dependent to some extent on the weather and the state of the ground and whether you have access to an indoor school. Ideally your weekly programme might be: Monday — dressage, followed by some work over cavalletti. Tuesday — hacking out, making use of lanes to practise moving

the horse away from your leg. Trotting up and down hill, walking through water, etc. Jump any small logs and ditches you find. Wednesday — dressage, followed by jumping exercise in your schooling area. Thursday — work outside again, perhaps spend twenty minutes or so on dressage in the corner of a flat field, then go for a long, steady trot around the fields, followed by a long, slow canter. If there are any small obstacles in your path, jump them. Friday — work over a small course of fences after a twenty-minute warm-up. Saturday — dressage, with perhaps some cavalletti work at the end, or take a long hack out after your dressage. Sunday — rest-day. If possible turn the horse out for an hour or two, or at the very least, lead him out for twenty minutes to nibble the grass and stretch his legs.

3. It is a good idea to give your horse ten minutes' grazing every day if you cannot turn him out.

How many fences to jump

1. At the start of training, when the jumps are very small, you can jump an almost unlimited number of times without harming or tiring the horse. At this stage you should be governed by the frame of mind of the horse; do not jump the same fences so many times that he becomes bored or sloppy. Jump until he is going really well, and then stop.

2. When the fences reach three feet you should cut down the number of actual jumps considerably. Twelve to twenty fences in one session will be plenty unless you are jumping a course. The course will probably consist of eight fences, and the first round can usually be improved. You may need to work some of the fences individually and the combinations two or three times, and then work the course once or twice more until you get it right. Always finish on a good note.

3. If things are not going well you may be over-facing your horse by having built too difficult a course. In this case select just three or four fences — perhaps on an easy circuit around the arena — and jump these again two or three times until you get a satisfactory result. If on the other hand the horse has jumped only six or seven obstacles but has done it very well, in a balanced manner with no difficulties, reward him by finishing and taking him out to cool off on a quiet ride.

4. As with all training, it is easy to overdo jumping and sour the horse by endless repetition. Knowing when to stop is just as

Trot approach	Pony	Horse
one stride	16–18'	18–21'
two strides	28–30'	30–32'
three strides	38–40'	40–42'

Canter approach	Pony	Horse
one stride	20–22'	22–24'
two strides	30–32'	32–35'
three strides	40–42'	42–45'
No-stride bounce	9–10'	11–12'

Trotting poles	4'	4' 6"–5'

Diagram 23a Gymnastic jumping, distances between fences

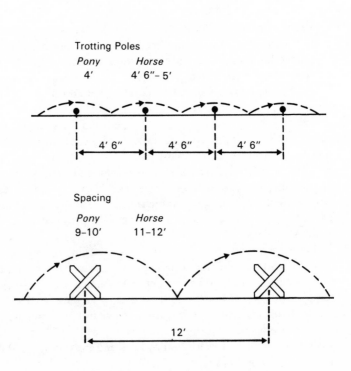

Trotting Poles

Pony	Horse
4'	4' 6"– 5'

4' 6"   4' 6"   4' 6"

Spacing

Pony	Horse
9–10'	11–12'

12'

Diagram 23b Non-jumping bounce – canter approach

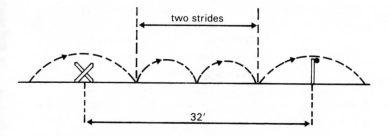

Trot approach to Cavalletti followed by two canter strides to rail

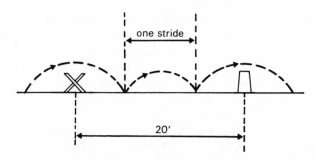

Trot approach to Cavalletti followed by one canter stride to hog's back

Diagram 23c

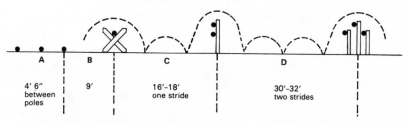

A Trotting poles (at least three) spaced 4′ 6″–5′ apart.
B Cavalletti, 9′ from third trotting pole, 1′ 6″ high.
C Upright with two rails spaced 16′–18′ from cavaletti, 2′ 6″ high.
D Spread jump (hog's back), 30′–32′ from upright, 2′ 9″–3′ high.

Diagram 23d

important as knowing when to go on, and perhaps more difficult. The horse does learn by repetition, but he also learns by associating a particular action of his with a pleasant and comfortable reaction from his rider. So it is good to associate in his mind the pleasant result of stopping work when his action has been a succession of particularly good jumps.

5. The final jump in any training session is the most important one. The memory of this jump stays with the horse and exerts a strong influence on his training, regardless of what happened earlier in the lesson.

Suitable jumping exercises and courses

1. Keep in mind exactly what you want to achieve in each lesson. Your goal in jumping is to bring your horse to a state of self-carriage, so that he approaches his fences balanced and jumps easily, off his hocks, without undue strain or excitement.

2. Perform your warm-up around your fences, and during the warm-up trot the horse over one or two small fences when he is perhaps not expecting to jump. This is very useful with a horse who is inclined to rush.

3. Using trotting poles or cavalletti on their lowest height, and one or more small cross-rails, you can develop several trotting exercises combining circles with trotting over small fences from different directions.

4. Take care that your horse performs all circles and corners accurately, and that you always take a straight approach line to the centre of each fence.

5. To teach your horse to judge his own correct take-off zone, and also to prepare him for angling fences later on, set up a fence (a very small parallel) in the centre of the arena. Ride a figure of eight, jumping the fence on a slightly diagonal line to join your two circles. Your horse will still be kept straight from the centre of the fence, and also straight between your legs and your hands with his hind-quarters directly behind his head, but he will jump the fence at a slight angle instead of at 90°.

6. After working the above exercise in trot, try it in a canter. Jumping out of a trot the horse can take off more or less at any time, but from the canter he must learn how to position himself and get his timing right. He must be more accurate, and be able to judge the height of the fence correctly. He will also learn to change his canter lead over the fence in preparation for the change of direction a few strides after the fence.

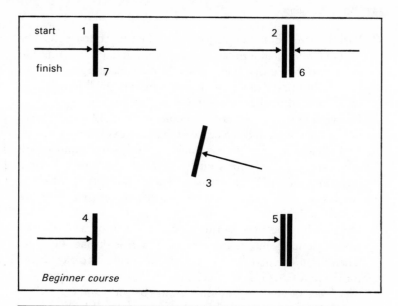

Beginner course

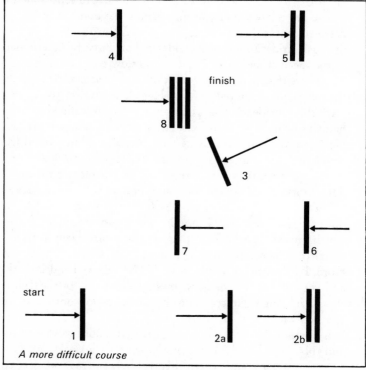

A more difficult course

Diagram 24 Simple jumping courses

7. Early courses should be very simple. The first course should be nothing more than four fences round the outside of the ring. Go around to the right, change across the diagonal and go around to the left, but first make sure the fences are very small and are built to be jumped in either direction.

8. Progressing to slightly more difficult courses, place your fences in from the wall, and include one fence across the diagonal.

9. There is an almost unlimited number of fairly simple courses you can design and build for your horse. Make the course flowing, offer no acute angles and no places where the rider would have to check back too hard or turn too sharply to get to a fence. See sample diagram 24.

10. On the day you plan to ride a course, warm up around your fences, jumping maybe one or two in a trot during warm-up. Then jump the first fence — perhaps reducing it to a cross-rail for the first two or three jumps and then building it back up. The first fence of any course should always be small and easy. Then jump the first and second fences in a canter. All fences in any course are related, and you must know the number of strides between fences. For example, from fence No.1 to No.2 may be five easy strides (number of strides will of course be determined by the speed of the canter, but keep to a slow, easy canter at first). Make sure that your horse goes sufficiently relaxed to take only the five strides required. If he is sluggish he may try to put in a sixth short stride, or if he is being hurried, or is inclined to rush, he may try to make it in four. After working fences No.1 and No.2 practise No.3 and No.4 together, and so on around the course. Practise particularly any combinations with one or two strides between them, since these will be the most difficult.

11. After working all parts of the course individually, you are ready to take the course as a whole. If you have any particular difficulties in the round practise the combinations of fences which caused the problems, then try the course again. If things go fairly well give the horse a break and then try the course once more. By this time everything should be balanced and smooth, and you can reward the horse by finishing work for the day. If things are not right continue the work session until you are satisfied with the results.

12. It is obvious that jumping a course is a strenuous work session, and this should be done not more than once a week.

13. Once you are in competition fairly regularly you may not need to

work courses at home at all. You may want to spend your jumping schooling sessions at home, concentrating on something the horse finds difficult — for example, combinations, or other related distances — rather than jumping actual courses.

14. When you are jumping courses remember to take particular care in the corners. Negotiating corners correctly is often difficult, since the horse knows more fences lie ahead and is keen to get to them, but correct cornering provides you with straight, accurate approaches to the fences, and this is the key to jumping clean. If the corner is poorly performed you may lose the hind-quarters, and therefore your 'engine' will not be in a position to propel you over the fence.

15. Combinations should be introduced fairly early in your horse's jumping training, provided they are kept small and the distances are easy. For a one stride in and out, a distance of 24 ft is only correct if you approach in canter at 12 miles per hour! For a green horse, approaching more slowly, 21 feet will probably be a comfortable one stride and 33 feet a comfortable two strides, even though later you will need 36 feet for two strides.

16. Whenever you ride a combination, whether it is two, three or more jumping efforts, approach completely straight and balanced. If you get the first fence right you should be right all the way through. Make sure you jump straight over the centre of each fence. Sit into the horse, and drive more than you would for a single fence and do not look *at* the fences, but look *up, over* the centre of the *last* fence in the line.

17. Jumping in a confined space — i.e., an indoor arena or small schooling area — is much more difficult for the horse than jumping outside in a nice big field or across country. This is yet another reason for keeping your show-jumping fences very small at the start of jumping training and increasing their size only gradually as the horse gains confidence and suppleness.

Jumping problems and remedies

1. Problems, such as refusing or running out, do not just suddenly happen. For the observant and knowledgeable trainer there are many early-warning signals. The sensitive trainer will take immediate action to put things right before they go really wrong.

2. Early signs that all is not well include the horse putting in a short stride just in front of the jump; not jumping straight across the

centre of the fence and continuing in a straight line; sudden turns to left or right just before take-off; jumping one side of the fence instead of the centre; turning sharply left or right on landing; changing leads at the canter on the approach to the fence; rushing the fence; bucking over the fence, or on landing or kicking back in the air or after jumping; getting over-excited; raising his head out of the angle of control; taking off much too early and throwing himself at the fence; and snatching at the bit and diving his head down repeatedly.

3. These problems may be due to one or several of a variety of reasons. First, there may simply be lack of sufficient training or over-facing. Do not ask a horse to jump fences which are too big or too difficult for his stage of training. He may alternatively have suffered a fall, and consequently lost confidence, or be weak and lack sufficient condition to jump comfortably. He may be suffering pain — perhaps from the saddle or bridle, or from the rider.

4. Quite frequently the rider is at fault. He may be shortening the stride too much on the approach, interfering with the horse as he tries to jump, presenting him badly, not riding the corner before the fence and the approach line correctly, or simply lack determination or ability.

5. It is important for the rider to be good enough to stay in balance with the horse when jumping. If the rider gets ahead of the horse, or behind him, he will hamper him by dropping him in front of the fence or making the balance problem too difficult for him. The rider must not look down at the fence on the approach; he should look up, straight over the centre of it. The rider must use sufficient driving aids at the appropriate time, and must not over-ride the horse. Above all, the rider must give the horse freedom of his head over the fence and not hit him in the teeth with the bit or get towed over the fence on the reins.

6. The first step to effecting a cure of any problem with the horse's jumping is correct diagnosis of the cause of the trouble. After that, use your common sense. If the problem is lack of training, go back to the lunge-line if necessary. If the problem is the rider, get more experience and instruction on older, made horses, before attempting to train a youngster over fences.

7. As with all training, with jumping in particular it is important to set things up so that situations work for you instead of against

you. For instance, if you know the horse to be sticky at a particular obstacle, jump him towards home instead of away from home, and have an experienced horse with you to give you a lead over if necessary.

8. Never attempt to jump at all until you have the horse moving freely and calmly forward between your legs and your hands, and take great care that fences are placed so that it is easy for him to get to them straight and balanced.

Walking the course

1. In a three-day event, as soon as you have passed the veterinary panel your horse can be handed over to your groom to be tidied up and have his mane plaited for the parade of competitors, and you can inspect the show-jumping course at that time.

2. Walk the course as many times as is necessary to learn it perfectly. Assess the problems carefully, and remember that your horse may be a little tired and not capable of his usual athletic ability.

3. If the competition is a one-day event the order of phases is usually i) dressage, ii) show-jumping, iii) cross-country. This is much easier for the horse and more convenient for the rider and the groom, since the horse should be clean and have his mane plaited for both dressage and show-jumping, but his mane should be left loose for cross-country.

4. Learn the course, and assess the problems carefully. It is likely to be flowing and straightforward at a one-day event, without any trick distances.

5. For show-jumping the horse must jump with much more precision and accuracy than is required on cross-country. Your preparation should keep this in mind. However, the dressage phase will have provided you with a warm-up and with the cross-country to follow; do not over-work your horse when preparing him for the show-jumping phase.

6. There are a few one-day events where the order of events will be the same as for a three-day event. In this case you must take extra care in your warm-up. Work the horse systematically over the practice fences so that he appreciates that he must jump cleanly and carefully.

7. The horse will jump in the arena with greater care if he has not already been round the cross-country course at speed.

Riding the show-jumping course

1. Whether the competition is a one-day or a three-day, the horse must be alert and responsive before he is ready to go into the show-jumping arena.

2. At a one-day event this will require a minimum of fifteen minutes' warm-up. Probably, if he is relatively inexperienced, he will require longer.

3. Jump the practice fences a few times as a vertical and a few times as a spread. Make sure the horse is alert and responsive.

4. If you are prepared too soon and have to wait around to enter the ring your horse will become bored and lose interest. So judge your timing carefully and use your warm-up time well.

5. Ride the course with calm determination, sticking as close as you can to the line you determined when you walked the course.

6. In a three-day event you will have to parade with the other competitors before the jumping competition. After the parade prepare your horse for the precision and accuracy that are required now. He must change his style from the previous day, when he was encouraged to stand off his fences and jump them at speed. Use the practice fences, first as an upright post and rails to ensure your horse has no stiffness left from the previous day's efforts. Then jump the upright as a single rail. If the horse does hit it jump it again, and he will probably realize that it needs more precision, and jump clean the second time. Reward him and change the fence to a parallel. Repeat the same procedure.

7. Keep your horse alert as you wait for your turn. His hind-quarters should be well engaged underneath him, and he should remain completely responsive to your aids. When it is your turn go into the arena and salute the judges and wait for the signal to start your round. In a three-day event the course will be long and twisty, so ride it with determination and care, keeping to the track you determined when you walked round it.

8. Time is a considerable factor, and you cannot afford to swing wide on the corners. You must keep up a steady pace without hurrying, and ride the course with a cool head, using all your ability to help your horse.

9. In a three-day event the starting order for the jumping is usually in reverse order of the placings, so that the horse at the bottom of the list is first into the arena, and the leading horse and rider jumps last. You will know your final placing almost as soon as you have jumped, and the prizes are presented immediately after

the leading horse has completed his round. You will be required to be mounted for the prize-giving (if you have won or are placed), so it may be necessary for you and your horse to wait around for a while. If the weather is bad make sure you provide adequate protection for your horse (in the shape of a wool cooler, blanket, or rain sheet), and do not let him get chilled while standing around.

10. After the show-jumping return the horse to the stables and either prepare him for the journey home or settle him down for a well-earned rest. Put a cooling lotion on his legs before bandaging them. If his mane is plaited carefully undo the braids and brush it out. Brush him off, and put on appropriate rugs or blankets, depending on the weather.

11. After an event the horse will need an easy week at home. Give only walking exercise, and maybe half an hour's grazing each day. Remember to adjust his food accordingly.

12. The following week he can return to his training programme if the event season continues. If it is the close of the season he can be roughed off gradually, and be turned out when the weather permits.

PART FIVE
Count-down to competition

A graduated get-fit programme

1. The process of getting a horse fit is gradual and systematic, just like his dressage and jumping training. The three-day event horse must be as fit as a top racehorse, and also so well trained and mentally stable that he can produce a calm, accurate dressage test when he is at peak fitness.

2. The training programme to get the horse fit for a one-day event will take eight to twelve weeks. He will require daily dressage and road-work, some jumping practice, and during the last few weeks some fast work to develop lungs and heart. Complete details are given in Part Two of this book.

3. The horse starts his first year of eventing with novice competitions. If he has been well schooled and is properly fit he is likely to gain sufficient points to move up a grade by the end of the season. If the horse is ready for the bigger, more difficult fences, this is fine, but make sure he has at least four runs in the novice division before you allow him to gain the points which will up-grade him.

4. All horses will benefit greatly from being given an 'easy' run their first time out. Less experienced riders would be wise to remain as novices for at least six events.

5. Even after your horse starts to compete in horse trials he should continue his general education by entering hunter and jumper competitions at horse shows and going to dressage shows. This will help him to accept travelling and strange surroundings as a matter of course.

6. Choose your events carefully, and take particular notice of the dates by which the entries must be posted. Fill out the forms well in advance, and keep them safely so that they are ready to be posted on the opening date.
7. Learn the dressage tests thoroughly.
8. A horse should be capable of taking part in one event a week (one-day events) on average. He will probably be feeling pretty good the day after he has made a big effort, but the day after that he will be at a lower ebb, and should be given a very easy time that day.
9. The horse needs a complete break after the eventing season of from three to six weeks.
10. At the start of the following season the horse should compete in as many events as possible, with the aim of preparing him for his first three-day event. You should not expect your horse to compete in more than two three-day events in this, his second year of eventing. One of these should be at the end of the spring season and the other in the autumn. The horse may not have time for a complete rest in the summer but he should certainly have four easy, very relaxed weeks.
11. The next full year of competition will set the pattern to be followed with an advanced event horse. The goals will be two big three-day events, one in spring and the other in the autumn.
12. Only a mentally well-balanced horse of strong constitution is likely to remain in top eventing for more than a few years. You must guard against the horse growing tired and stale; he cannot remain at peak fitness from March until October, but if you plan the year carefully, giving him four weeks' break in the early summer and six to eight weeks' rest in the winter, you will be giving him the best possible chance of a long and successful career.

Prepare for the dressage test

1. Your horse will have learned all the movements required in your training programme but he must be used to working in an actual arena. Mark out the correct-size arena, define the corners, put up letters and know the test thoroughly yourself.
2. Learn the tests well in advance and ride them in an arena often enough to ensure that you know them. Either use a different horse or ride at walk, or trot, so that the horse you are going to ride in competition does not learn the test and anticipate.

3. Practise entering the arena from A to C on a sawdust line. Also practise on a painted white line on grass, if possible, so that your horse will be accustomed to trotting straight along it, and will not shy from a cross at X or a large dot at G.

4. Practise the salute. It should not be hurried. Keep your back straight and your head up as you enter the arena. Establish a square halt. Take the reins in the left hand and, if you are a man, take off your hat in a long, sweeping gesture. Remember to keep the palm of your hand towards the horse's flank. Replace the hat equally smoothly, take the reins in both hands, make sure your horse is listening, and move off on a straight line. Women salute by taking the reins in the left hand and moving the right arm in a clear and precise movement so that it lies in a straight line parallel with the body. Bow slightly from the hips with back straight and head low. Make graceful, unhurried movements. Straighten up, bring the right hand back to the reins and prepare to move off.

5. Always end your dressage practice work sessions with a square halt on the centre-line, then move off with a loose rein, as you would from the final halt of a dressage test.

Hints on riding the dressage test

1. Be very conscious of your horse's straightness on the long sides of the arena. You can lose marks for allowing the quarters to fall even slightly to the inside or to the outside.

2. In canter transitions, particularly if you are moving away from the judge, show a little inside flexion. Without this flexion it looks to the judge as if your horse's head is slightly bent to the outside.

3. Show correct length-bend on the circles and in all corners and turns.

4. Ride the test accurately and with confidence. Remember to make frequent half-halts — at least before corners and transitions.

Prepare for the show-jumping

1. Take part in schooling shows and show-jumping compeitions at the lower levels.

2. The show-jumping phase of an event is not difficult, but it should not be neglected. Adequate experience at small shows is important.

Prepare for the cross-country

1. It is impossible to prepare at home for all the possibilities of a cross-country course.
2. Introduce your horse to all the usual fences. If he is jumping willingly over ditches and water, and can cope with different distances in combinations, jumping into a water splash, and up and down a small bank you should have no problems.
3. Horses learn cross-country by competing at actual events. If his dressage is right and his show-jumping is right, his cross-country will be good.

Count-down to Event Day

1. *5 to 7 days before the event:*
   a) Check your horse's shoes. Make sure they are not worn thin, and that the thread in the stud-holes is in good shape. Pack holes with oiled cotton-wool.
   b) Check your tack. See that it is in good order, and nothing needs to be repaired.
   c) Check your clothing. See that everything you need is clean and in good repair.
   d) Draw up a list of everything you need to take with you, and check that everything is available. Do not leave this to the last minute. It is a good plan to have a permanent list which can be used as a basic guide. (See sample lists following.)
2. *4 days before the event:*
   a) Plan your journey. Decide how long it will take you to travel to the event, and what route you will follow. Allow plenty of time. Your aim is to arrive in the early afternoon the day before the event.
   b) If the distance is such that you cannot arrive before the close of declarations, send a letter or telegram to reach the secretary before the specified time.
   c) Check your vehicle: tyre pressures, petrol, oil, etc. Check your trailer: tyre pressures, electrical hook-up, hitch, etc.
3. *The day before you leave home:*
   a) Trim horse if necessary. Remove whiskers from around muzzle, trim long hair off legs (with comb and scissors), tidy up ears (do not clip out the inside of the ears; simply clip down the edge to give sharp definition).

b) Check that the mane and tail are well pulled and clean. If necessary shampoo mane and tail with pure soap or a safe animal shampoo.

c) Pack your vehicle, checking off your list as you go. It is an excellent idea to have a tack trunk for your horse, and a small first-aid box which remains in your vehicle.

On arrival at the location of the event

1. Go to the Secretary's office and confirm that your horse will compete. Collect your numbers, maps and official programme.
2. If there is to be an official course walk with the Technical Delegate, join this. This will make certain that you do not miss any fences and that you know of all compulsory flags, while it also allows you to ask any questions you may have.
3. There may be several classes or divisions; make certain you know which coloured markers apply to the obstacles for your division.
4. Concentrate on the individual fences first, and then on the overall pattern. (See specific instructions on walking the course in Part Three.)
5. Pay attention to the terrain and the approach to each fence. If the going varies over the course remember where it is good and where it is bad.
6. Check out the landing side of each fence to make sure you have a good landing if you jump the fence from the take-off point you have selected. If your horse is competing for the first time give him every chance by choosing the easiest way round.
7. If your horse is more experienced, generally speaking, the straightforward fences may be angled if it will save time. Do not angle a fence if this will make it far wider or more difficult — e.g., a spread.
8. If your horse is excitable his first run over a cross-country course is very important. He will be more likely to settle sensibly to his job if you take him slowly.
9. Assess the individual fences and decide where the problems lie. Decide how you intend to negotiate each fence and stick to the decision, even if you learn other competitors will jump it in a different way.
10. Measure the distances in combination fences carefully, and decide the necessary speed of approach to negotiate the obstacle with easy striding.
11. Ride in your horse. It is a good idea to give him an opportunity of

seeing the grounds, and he will be less likely to be excited by the strange surroundings the next day. Work him through his dressage test as near as you can to the actual arenas, but be sure you do not ride in any unauthorized place (e.g., in the arenas themselves, in the show-jumping ring, on the cross-country course), as this would be grounds for elimination.

12. Keep your horse calm and obedient and totally responsive to your aids. Do not excite him, or let him get the idea that this is an exciting place. Ride for an hour or more until he is producing good work.

13. Find your stabling, if you have not already settled your horse in there before walking the course. Make sure your horse has plenty of bedding, and that there is nothing in his box which could injure him. Make sure he is well groomed and that the stud-holes in his shoes are cleaned out and tapped. Plug with oily cotton-wool so you will have no trouble inserting the studs next day.

14. Give your horse his water and a hay-net and leave him for half an hour to get used to his surroundings. He can have a small feed as soon as he is settled. If he is very relaxed give him his normal tea-time feed.

15. Clean the tack and put everything ready for the competition. If the horse is to wear bandages instead of boots, put these ready, together with fresh gamgee padding. Crepe bandages are best, as they will 'give' on the legs and yet they afford good support.

16. If you did not bring water from home, fill your water-carriers in case you do not have time to go for water the next day.

17. Fill your second hay-net — this is for your horse after he has finished the event.

18. At 10.0 p.m. give your horse his night feed. If you have an early riding time, take away his hay-net for the night. Even if your riding time is not too early, your horse will not need much hay. You want his stomach clear of bulk, or he will have trouble galloping without stress.

On the morning of the event

1. Groom the horse, plait his mane, and if you have to trailer to the grounds from the stabling bandage his legs in preparation for the journey.

2. Water and feed your horse, but do not give him hay. Leave his loose-box clean and tidy.

3. If you have not already collected your number cloth do so immediately you arrive at the event location.
4. Prepare for your dressage test. Unplug the stud-holes in your horse's shoes and insert the studs most suitable for the going in the dressage arena. Wearing studs will give your horse much more confidence, and he will be able to go deeper into the corners and show more marked changes of pace, as he will not be afraid of slipping.
5. Work the horse through dressage warm-up in the same place that you rode the day before. Remember to take off his tail bandage and give him a final wipe-over a few minutes before you are due to start your test.
6. Enter the dressage area as the previous competitor is leaving and trot round the outside of the arena. Use the time before the judges ring the bell to make a few transitions and changes of direction. When the bell rings make sure your horse is on the bit, and make a straight approach line before you enter at A.
7. Try to smile as you salute, and remain calm and confident throughout the test. At the end salute and then walk straight forward on a loose rein, make a smooth half-circle towards the long side and continute to walk quietly until you leave the arena at A. You may then pat your horse, dismount, and give him a titbit.
8. Cool off your horse, and you may wash out his mouth or allow him one or two swallows of water, but do not give him anything to eat or drink. Remove the tack and keep him warm and dry (you can put him back into your trailer if you like) until it is time to prepare for the show-jumping.
9. Make sure you are ready in plenty of time for the show-jumping, and have made any necessary adjustments to the horse's tack. Mount and assume your jumping seat right away. Find the practice fence and prepare for the jumping.
10. After the jumping phase again wash out your horse's mouth, cool him off and put him back in the trailer as soon as possible. He still must have nothing to eat or drink.
11. Change into your cross-country sweater and crash helmet and make any additions or alterations to your tack. Get your washing-down equipment ready and leave them by your trailer.
12. Ride your horse quietly down to the start of the cross-country, at a walk, ten minutes before your time. Check that the phase is

running on time. If so, give your horse a short, sharp gallop somewhere you will not interfere with anyone else and then return to the start. It will probably not be necessary to use the warm-up fence, since you have just done the show-jumping, but if you feel you need to take a couple of fences before going to the start allow yourself five minutes' extra time.

13. The starter will tell you when there are two minutes to go. Keep moving about quietly, but do not enter the starting-box until the 30-second warning. The starter will count down from five seconds, and you should be away immediately at a fast canter towards the first fence.

14. Ride calmly and with strong determination. Follow the track you decided on when walking the course, and encourage or steady your horse as and when necessary. Concentrate on every single fence; do not look for your friends in the crowd, and do not let anything distract you. You cannot afford to relax until you have passed through the finish flags. Remember to weigh in if this applies.

15. You and your horse should enjoy yourselves thoroughly if you complete the course without trouble. Dismount and loosen the girth, and make much of your horse. Walk him quietly for a few minutes until he stops blowing. Some events provide a vet at the finish to check the horses after they come off the cross-country and again after ten minutes of cooling out. This is not a requirement but is a service provided by the event organizers to help to ensure the well-being of all the horses participating.

16. If there is no veterinary check return to your trailer, remove your tack and bandages, and wash your horse down. Look for any cuts or injuries, and attend to them right away. Walk him dry, put cooling lotion on his legs and then gamgee and bandages. Put on a string sweat-sheet under his rug or blanket. Take out his studs and repack the stud-holes with oily cotton-wool. You may allow him one or two small mouthfuls of water as you are cooling him down, but do not give him a real drink until he is cool, dry and loaded back in the trailer.

17. A double handful of glucose powder in his first drink of water will help to restore lost energy and keep him happy. He can now have his hay-net. Try not to leave him in the trailer long before taking him home. He will not really rest until he gets to his own loose-box.

18. Make sure that your horse knows how happy you are with him,

and how much you enjoyed yourself. This can greatly influence his future performance.

19 When you arrive home it is a good idea to have a boiled feed waiting for your horse. This is a special treat, and is also easy to digest, and relaxing. Check him over once more and then leave him to rest for the night.

20. The next day he should be walked out in hand to get rid of any stiffness, and the following day he can be ridden quietly for half an hour.

21. The third day he should be back in full training.

The three-day event

1. Preparation for a three-day event involves extending the twelve-week training programme by a further four weeks. The horse must be at peak fitness, and will only have reached it if he has completed the programme without missing more than the odd day.

2. Three-day events generally take place from Friday to Sunday, but all the big events now require four days, Thursday to Sunday, to accommodate the large entry. Thursday and Friday will be dressage days, Saturday will be cross-country, and Sunday will be the parade of competitors and the final show-jumping. Often the larger events put on show-jumping competitions quite separate from the event competition in the morning of the Sunday and then hold the event show-jumping in the afternoon.

3. Even for a small three-day event you need to arrive at the location of the event by Wednesday afternoon — and Tuesday afternoon would be preferable — to give your horse time to settle down in the new surroundings.

4. It is possible to be both groom and rider and compete in one-day events, although it is much more fun to have a friend or groom along to help. For three-day eventing it is absolutely essential to have someone else to look after your horse.

5. Make sure your horse's shoes are in good order a week or so before leaving home, but even so, take along a spare set of shoes and an easy-boot in case you need them.

6. Check your list carefully so that nothing is left behind.

7. On the days preceding the event the horse should have his normal work. He will settle down and eat properly if his ordinary routine is followed. Try not to excite him or upset him in any way.

8. All three-day events hold a competitors' briefing, and it is absolutely essential for you to attend this, to concentrate closely on the information you are being given, and to ask any questions which you have, even if you are afraid your question might sound silly. Quite likely someone else had the same question but was afraid to ask.

9. You will be given a programme and a map of the speed and endurance phase, and then you will be driven round phases A and C and you will walk the steeplechase course.

10. Take note of the compulsory turning flags, or checkpoints on the roads and tracks, and mark off the kilometre signs on your map.

11. Walk the steeplechase course carefully. Usually it will consist of five fences on a circular loop, and each fence is jumped twice. You must work out the exact half-way point so that you can check your speed during the competition.

12. Walk the cross-country phase to gain an overall impression. (See specific instructions in Part Three.)

13. There is a veterinary check late in the afternoon of the day before the start of dressage — i.e., Wednesday afternoon if dressage starts Thursday, or Thursday afternoon if dressage does not start until Friday. Your horse needs to complete his exercise for that day and then be groomed ready for the veterinary inspection, so you will not have a great deal of time to spend on the cross-country course at this time.

14. The veterinary inspection is merely a formality unless your horse is definitely lame. Three-day-eventing is a risky sport on a sound horse, and it would be most unwise to start on an animal whose soundness was suspect.

15. After the veterinary check, make sure the stud-holes are cleaned out in your horse's shoes and replugged with oily cotton-wool. Tell your groom the exact time you want your horse the next day.

16. Experience will tell you how much work the horse needs before his dressage test. There are many different theories on how best to prepare for the dressage test but you will probably do best if you stick to your normal routine for warming up before this phase. Keep calm and try to convey to your horse a sense of confidence.

17. After the dressage test put on boots or bandages and your cross-country tack and give your horse a half-mile gallop at three-

quarter speed. Choose a place well away from the dressage area so that you do not disturb other competitors. This gallop will clear your horse's wind in preparation for the speed and endurance phase next day.

18. You have the rest of the day to walk the cross-country course again as many times as necessary and to check any short-cut routes you may be considering in any of the phases. Be very careful about taking short cuts. Your route must not miss any of the flags or checkpoints, and, of course, it must not be clogged with spectators. Usually short cuts are impossible on the cross-country, because the course is roped off to avoid the spectators getting in the way of the horses. However, short cuts are occasionally possible on phase A or C, but they must be very carefully checked.

19. More than one helper or groom can be of enormous assistance on speed and endurance day. Make certain that your groom or grooms are thoroughly briefed as to their duties. They must know the whereabouts of the start of each phase, and the 'vet-box' or 'pocket' at the finish of phase C. The compulsory ten-minute break and veterinary inspection takes place in this area, and all your washing-down equipment and spare tack must be taken there before the start of the speed and endurance phase.

20. Your groom can lead your horse to the start of phase A for you, and as soon as you have started should go directly to the 'vet-box' or 'pocket' to await your return from phase C.

21. If you have a second helper send him or her to the finish of phase A (which is also the start of phase B) in case you need any help getting into the starting-box for the steeplechase. This helper can also be waiting for you at a point about 500 m beyond the finish of phase B if you wish to check your horse over quickly before continuing on phase C.

22. Work out your times for roads and tracks, steeplechase and cross-country and write yourself a time schedule for the entire test. Make two copies of your schedule on post-cards ready to be strapped to your arms before the start of phase A. Make another card with your actual starting time for phase A and the time you intend to finish phase C, and how long you have in the 'vet-box' for washing down and cooling your horse. Give this to your groom, and make sure that he has a watch, synchronized to official event time.

23. Your time schedule might look something like this:

Start A	12.00	
1 km	12.03.25 sec	
2 km	12.06.30	22 minutes
3 km	12.09.45	3¼ min each km
4 km	12.13.00	
5 km	12.16.15	
Finish A	12.18	
In Hand	4.00	
Start B	12.22.00	
½ way	12.24.30	No penalties:
¾ way	12.26.45	5 min 13 sec
Finish B	12.27.13	
Start C	12.27.13	
1 km	12.34.00	
2 km	12.37.25	
3 km	12.40.50	
4 km	12.44.15	
5 km	12.47.40	34 minutes
6 km	12.51.05	
7 km	12.54.25	
8 km	12.57.50	
Finish C	13.01.13	
Compulsory		
Halt	10.00	
In Hand	2.00	
Start D	13.13.13	

24. Check on your horse again at evening feed-time. Make sure he is comfortable, and that bandages and boots and tack are clean and ready for the next day. Instruct the groom to remove the small hay-net at 10.0 p.m. if there is any hay left.

Speed and endurance day

1. First thing in the morning, check on whether there has been any change in the going since you walked the course. Rain in the night will probably have changed dry but low-lying areas into deep mud and swollen streams, and changed some simple take-off into a difficult one. If there has been a change in the going walk at least the most difficult parts of the course again, and

make any necessary decisions on whether to alter your line of approach at any of the fences.

2. Find out everything possible about how the early horses on the course are coping. How the course is jumping, which fences are proving most difficult, and so on. Do not alter your own plan of how to ride the course unless you realize that you had overlooked something and a change in tactics is wise. Remain calm and determined.

3. Take your saddle and weigh out on the scales at the starter's tent.

4. Tape one time schedule to your forearm, where you can read it easily as you go along. Put the other in a pocket in case you should have a fall and lose the schedule on your arm.

5. Strap on your watches, preferably one with a large, clear face and a minute hand and the other a wrist stop-watch. It is a good precaution to have a third watch, in your pocket, in case of emergency.

6. Make sure all your equipment is taken to the 'vet-box' at the end of phase C. Equipment should include three buckets, two sponges, glucose powder, several towels, four stable rubbers folded crosswise, if your horse is wearing bandages. These are to be tied just below the horse's knees before he is washed down, and will prevent the bandages from getting wet. You will also need a string cooler, blanket or rug, sweat-scraper, spare set of shoes and easy-boot, spare girth and over-girth, a whip, stirrup leathers and reins, a spare set of boots and bandages, and a spray to treat any cuts. For yourself you will want a cold drink, extra gloves, a towel and a coat. These things should be placed in a previously agreed position in the vet-box well before you are due to ride.

7. Check that your tack is correctly fitted. Making a single plait in the mane just behind the ears and securing the bridle to it can prevent the bridle being pulled off if you have a fall.

8. Have the horse walked to the start of phase A, wearing a rug, to arrive there ten minutes before your starting time.

9. When you arrive at the start of phase A ask the starter for a time check and then set your watches back the appropriate number of minutes, so that your starting-time falls exactly on 12.

10. Phase A is your warm-up, so you need only mount a few minutes before the off, tighten your girths and you are ready for the endurance phase.

Sample lists of equipment to take to the event
Use this as a base and add to it. Pin it up in your tack-room for easy
reference. Most events require an overnight stay and a considerable
journey.

Feed and utensils
Hay
Grain
Bran
Vitamins and additives
Two hay-nets
Water-bucket
Feed-bucket
Spare bucket for washing horse
Feed measure
Double-ended snaps
Screw-eyes
Hammer and screwdriver

Stable tools
Fork
Shovel
Broom
Muck Sack or Muck Skip

Horse's tack and clothing
Dressage saddle, pad and girth (spare girth, stirrup leathers and reins)
Dressage bridle
Cross-country and jumping saddle with clean pad or numnah
Cross-country bridle
Tail bandage and head bumper (optional)
Brushing boots (plus spare pair)
Over-reach (bell) boots (plus spare pair)
Running martingale and rein stops
Rubber reins for cross-country
Breast plate
Circingle or over-girth
Weight cloth with sufficient lead (if applicable)
Night rugs
Day rugs

Fly sheet
Rain sheet
String type anti-sweat sheet
Wool cooler
Bandages (at least two sets of crepe for use in competition, also
  flannel stable bandages and shipping boots or bandages)
Gamgee, sponges, sweat-scraper, towels
Complete grooming kit
Plaiting (braiding) kit
Studs and tap
Spare set of shoes — with correct-size nails from your shoer
Water carriers
Easy-boot (just in case)

First-aid supplies
Commercial human first-aid kit to be kept in vehicle
Cloths, towels and disinfectant
Brace, liniment, and cooling lotion
Auromycetin spray (or similar wound dressing)
Animalintex or Kaolin poultice
Colic drench
Banamine (injectable) with syringes and needles
Myoquin
Scissors and wound dressings and bandages
Electrolytes

Equipment for the rider
Black jacket for dressage and show-jumping
Black velvet hard hat for dressage
Hair-nets
Breeches
White shirts and stocks (at least two of each)
Gloves for dressage
Gloves for cross-country
Black boots
Sweater for cross-country
Safety helmet and cover for cross-country
Long whip for dressage schooling
Regulation-length whip to use on cross-country and show-jumping
Spurs, with spare pair of straps
Watches and stop-watch
Rule-book

Pack all your horse's equipment neatly into tack trunks so that you know exactly where to find everything.

Know the rules of the governing body of the competition. Carry the rule-book with you so that you can check on any questions which arise in your mind.

Make the extra effort and turn yourself and your horse out perfectly. This makes a pleasing picture and gives an impression of competence and professionalism. Decide to keep up a high standard both for your horse and for yourself, and enjoy the wonderful sport of eventing.

Index

Advanced Level, 14, 17, 18, 109
Aids, application of the, 52
Appaloosa, 16
Arena: in training, 19–20; making an arena, 20–1; accustoming horse to, 20–1; riding school figures in, 22–47
Ascending oxer, 120, 121

Balance, 55, 59–60
Banks, 110, 111
Bathing the horse, 80–1
Beginner equitation over fences, 54
Bit, on the, 60, 61
Body-weight/feeding ratio, 89–90
Bots, 83
British Horse Society, levels of eventing recognized by, 14
Bullfinch, 110, 111

Canter, 44, 47
Cantering poles, 54
Cavalletti, 54, 60, 129, 159
Change of rein: across the diagonal, 27, 29; within the circle, 27; half-circle and, 32, 38
Circles, in dressage, 54; 20-metre, 22–4; 10-metre, 25, 35, 39; 6-metre, 25, 39
Clothing for competition, correct, 64, 65, 66
Coffin fences, 112, 129–132

Collected gait, 47
Collection, 55, 62–3
Combination fences, 54, 128–9
Combined events, 14
Competition, final preparation for, 169–84
Conditioning the horse, 69–107
Controlled boldness, testing of in cross-country, 110, 112
Counter-canter, 45
Counter change of hand, 27, 30
Course evaluation, in cross-country, 112
Cross-country: as part of three-day eventing, 13. See also Ditches, Fences, Roads and Tracks, Speed and endurance, Steeplechase, etc.
Cross-country course: walking, 113–17; riding, 117–19

Diet, 88–90, 92, 96–7
Distance, testing, in cross-country, 110
Ditches, 110, 111
Doubler, 27, 28
Dressage: as part of three-day event, 13; early training for, 19; the arena, 20–1; preparing a horse for competition, 21–2; the school figures, 22–47; sequence of training, 54–63;

correct saddlery and dress
for test, 63–4; execution
and judging of tests, 66–7;
final preparation for test,
170–1; hints on test, 171
Drops, 110, 111

Eventing, three-day: origin,
13; three phases of, 13;
levels, 14
Extended gait, 47

Feeding of horses, 72–7
Feet, care of horse's, and
shoeing, 84, 91, 92–3, 97
Fences, 110, 119–32;
combinations, 54, 128–9;
bullfinch, 110, 111;
trakehner, 111, 119; coffins,
112, 129–32; upright or
vertical, 119–20; spreads,
120–2; over ditches, water,
123–6; banks, steps and
drops, 127–8; in
show-jumping, 149–67
Figures of eight (large and
 ' small), 32, 33–4
'First' horse, 15–16
Fitness, programme for,
84–99
Floating (or rasping) teeth, 83
Frame, 55, 60, 63

Gaits, 44, 47, 58; modes, 47,
59
Get-fit programme,
graduated, 169–70. *See also*
Conditioning the horse
Grids, 53, 54, 129
Grooming of horses, 77–80,
94

Gymnastic exercises, 154–5,
159

Half-circle, 32, 35, 38
Half-pass, 32, 37, 44, 46, 62
Half-pirouette, 59
Half-turn, 44
Halt, 45; half-halt, 60
Hind-quarters, engaging, 44,
54, 59–60
Hog's back, 121, 159
Horse trials, 14, 112, 169

Impulsion, 55, 62
Intermediate Level, 14, 16,
109
Internal parasites of horse,
53–4. *See also* Bots, Worms
Interval training, 99–107;
definition, 99; application,
100; use of, 103–4; more
advanced application,
104–5; factors in
(D.V.I.A.R.), 105, 106

Jumping, 15, 53–4, 117–43;
into the dark, 132–3. *See
also* Show-jumping,
Steeplechase

Lane, jumping, 148–9
Lateral work, 53, 54
Leg-yielding, 37, 40
Levels in eventing, 14, 16, 17,
18
Long-reining over fences, 152
Loops, in serpentine, 32
Loose-jumping, 148, 152
Lungeing, 87, 150–1, 152

Medium gait, 47

Novice Level, 14

Olympic Games, 13
'Olympic' horse, 18
One-day events, 14, 112;
training programme for,
169
Outline, of a horse — *see*
Frame
Over-training, 107
Oxers: square, 15; ascending,
120, 121

Parallels, 120, 121, 122
Physiology of sustained
exertion, 99–100
Preliminary Level, 14, 16
Pulse — *see* Temperature/
Pulse/Respiration ratio

Quartering, 77

Rasping teeth — *see* Floating
Rein-back, 45, 59
Renvers (haunches-out), 37,
43, 62
Respiration — *see*
Temperature/Pulse/
Respiration ratio
Rhythm, 55, 57
Riding technique, 47–52; seat,
47–8; concentration and
relaxation, 49; balance,
49–50; suppleness, 50;
co-ordination and
confidence, 50–1; grip, 51;
'hands', 51–2; application of

the aids, 52; jumping, 53–4
Roads and tracks, as part of
three-day event, 13, 134–6,
139–40
Rule-book, importance of,
67–8

Saddle, position of, 48
Saddlery: correct for dressage
test, 63–4; for speed and
endurance test, 64; for
show-jumping test, 65; care
of, 65–6
School figures, in dressage:
circles, 22–5, 35, 39, 54;
turns, 25, 35, 44; doublers,
27, 29; change of rein,
27, 29; counter change of
hand, 27; figures of eight,
32, 33–4; serpentine, 32, 36;
half-circle and change of
rein, 32, 33; volte and
half-volte, 35; leg-yielding,
37; shoulder-in, 37; travers,
37; renvers, 37; half-pass,
44; counter-canter, 45; halt,
45; rein-back, 45;
transitions, 45–7; gaits, 47
Schooling, 19–22; school
figures, 22–47; routine,
60–1; in fitness training, 87,
94, 95
Seat, in riding, 48–9
'Second' horse, 16
Selecting a horse, 14–18;
'first' horse, 15–16; 'second'
horse, 16–17; 'Olympic'
horse, 18
Sequence of dressage training,
54–63
Serpentine, 32, 36
Shoulder-in, 37, 41, 59, 62

Show-jumping: as part of
three-day event, 13; correct
dress for test, 65; general
description of, 147–67; final
preparation for, 171
Show-jumping course:
walking, 165; riding, 166–7
Size, ideal, for event horse, 14
Speed and endurance: as part
of three-day event, 13;
Phases A–D (roads and
tracks, steeplechase,
cross-country) in, 13;
correct saddlery and dress
for, 64–5; general
description, 109–45. *See
also* Cross-country;
Ditches; Fences; Roads and
Tracks; Steeplechase etc.
Spreads (spread fences), 110,
111, 120–2; square oxer, 15;
ascending oxer, 120, 121;
parallels, 120, 121, 122;
hog's back, 121; triple bar,
120, 121, 122
Stable-management, good,
69–84; equipment, 69–70;
construction and fittings,
70–1; routine, 70–1; feeding
of horses, 72–7; grooming,
77–80; bathing, 80–1; care
of horses' teeth, 81–2;
digestive problems of horse,
82–3; its internal parasites,
83–4; care of feet and
shoeing, 84
Starting-box, 117–18
Steeplechase: as part of
three-day eventing, 13,
136–9
Stirrups, length of, 49
Stockholm Games (1912),
first three-day event at, 13
Straightness, 55, 61–2

Strapping, 78, 94
Suppleness, 55, 57–9; of rider,
50

Tack for competition,
correct, 63–4, 65–6
Teeth, care of horse's, 81–2
Temperature/Pulse/
Respiration ratio (TPR),
101–4
'Third' horse, 16–17
Thoroughbred, 16, 17
Three-Day Event: constituent
parts of, 13; preparation
for; 105–6; count-down to,
172–3; arrival at, 173–4;
morning of, 174–7; general
information on, 177–80;
speed and endurance day,
180; sample lists of
equipment for, 182–3
TPR — *see* Temperature/Pulse/
Respiration ratio
Training: objectives of, 52;
timetable for show-
jumping, 156–7
Training Level, 14, 17
Trakehner fences, 111, 119
Transitions, 45–7, 54; for
suppling the horse, 59
Travers (haunches-in), 37, 42,
44, 62
Triple bars, 120, 121, 122
Trot, 47
Trotting poles, 54, 148, 152,
153
Turning, testing in
cross-country, 110
Turns, 25, 26; on the
forehand, 35; on the
haunches, 44, 59, 62

United States Combined
Training Association, levels

of eventing recognized by,
14
Uprights, 110, 111, 119–120

Vet-box, 140–2
Veterinary inspection, 13,
140, 144–5
Volte and half-volte, 35, 39

Walk, 47
Water, and jumping, 110,
123–6
Whip, 56–7, 64, 65, 119
Working gait, 47
Worms, 83–4
Wynmalen, Henry, 52

Young Rider's Level, 14